THE NEWCASTLE GUIDE TO
HEALING WITH GEMSTONES

By the same authors:

THE NEWCASTLE GUIDE TO HEALING WITH
CRYSTALS: Balancing the Human Energy System
for Physical and Spiritual Well-Being

THE NEWCASTLE GUIDE TO
HEALING WITH GEMSTONES

How to Use Over Seventy Different Gemstone Energies

PAMELA LOUISE CHASE
&
JONATHAN PAWLIK

NEWCASTLE PUBLISHING CO., INC.
North Hollywood, California
1989

Edited by Jim Strohecker and Nancy Shaw
Cover/Book Design by Riley K. Smith
Illustrations by Nell Blackwell

First Edition April 1989

Grateful Acknowledgement is made to the following for permission to
reprint copyrighted material:

> DeVorss and Co.: Excerpts from *The Spiritual Value of Gemstones*,
> by Wallace G. Richardson and Lenora Huett, Copyright © 1980 by
> DeVorss and Co.

A Newcastle Book
First Printing April 1989
9   8   7   6   5   4
Printed in the United States of America

ACKNOWLEDGEMENTS

We wish to thank the people at Newcastle Publishing, and especially our editors Jim Strohecker and Nancy Shaw, for their sensitive and conscientious refinement of our manuscript.

We also extend our love and thanks to the Devas for their love and support, which is the foundation of this book and of our lives.

DISCLAIMER

This book is not intended to diagnose, prescribe, or treat any ailment, nor is it intended in any way as a replacement for medical consultation when needed. The author and publishers of this book do not guarantee the efficacy of any of the methods herein described, and strongly suggest that at the first suspicion of any disease or disorder the reader consult a physician.

CONTENTS

LISTS OF CHARTS AND ILLUSTRATIONS

PREFACE

Anyone who has had a pet knows the pure trust and love that an animal so freely shares. We often take this love for granted, not fully understanding how we are being served in this way. Nevertheless, we have been loved, healed, and cheered on by the devotion of our pets. It is time for us to understand that all living things have a Consciousness that gives and receives compassion, and that we are intimately connected with the Kingdoms of Nature through our mutual service to each other. Our aim in this book is to help you deepen your connection with Nature. Although this perspective is quite different from the way we as a culture currently perceive Nature, it is more in tune with the wisdom of the Native Americans. We also hope that you will learn to see stones as friends and guides rather than as inanimate objects to be taken for granted. When we admire the beauty in all things, including stones, we are also affirming Nature.

This book has been written to share the spiritual healing gifts of the Mineral Kingdom with those of you who are working on a daily basis with personal growth. We originally thought when we began work on this book that we would be involved in many different kinds of activities. Our plans "fell through," however, and instead we were sent in solitude to clean and beautify the houses of our own minds. It seemed like just when

I would get one dusty room of personal doubts tidied up, the dust would collect somewhere else. The purpose of this book is to aid you in the daily discipline of "housecleaning" your thoughts, and it includes affirmations as well as many other ways to incorporate gemstones to this end.

Jonathan and I turned to Nature, as we do when we are in solitude, and we opened ourselves to the healing of the stones. It took the intensity of solitude to learn what we needed to learn, and to write about it. Working with the stones was a journey of the Soul, and like the journey of the tarot Fool, we learned the lessons of many lifetimes. Our personal journey was filled with joy and a sense that all was unfolding according to plan.

The material in the text "in quotes" and in this typeface has been channeled through Jonathan by different Devas, which we consider to be the Higher Selves of the Kingdoms of Nature. We hope that you will also sense the joy and compassion of the Mineral Kingdom as you read, and find your own personal relationship with the stones.

Pamela Louise Chase

PART ONE

Exploring the
World of Gemstones

In the four chapters of Part One, we share some of the practices that helped develop our skills in understanding the qualities of gemstones. These practices take patience and are not learned overnight, but they are enjoyable and will help expand your intuitive understanding in other areas. Chapter 1 is an introduction to the physical qualities by which gemstones are identified. We have pondered over the possible parallels between the physical and spiritual qualities of gemstones, and we leave you to explore this issue. Chapter 2 deals with the spiritual aspects of gemstones and acquaints us with the unifying concept of life force energy and the human energy system. We introduce the Devas and discuss the central role of our personal beliefs in Spiritual perception and understanding of the Higher Realms. Finally, we review some basics of choosing and caring for gemstones. Chapter 3 describes three of the five perspectives from which we have learned about gemstones: color, sound, and chakra and subtle body affinities. Chapter 4 discusses two final perspectives on learning about gem energy: the three-step process of healing (also described in

1

The Newcastle Guide to Healing with Crystals) and the four elements of Nature. These five perspectives are the routes we took in developing our intuitive discrimination. We have detailed them in the hope that your own process may be made easier.

1 | Physical Aspects of Gemstones

DEFINITIONS

In this chapter we will get acquainted with gemstones by taking a look at how gemologists study and identify their physical properties. We will begin by defining some terms. A *mineral* is a naturally occurring inorganic solid having a definite chemical composition and an internal structure that is geometrically uniform. Most of the stones that we will talk about in this book are *minerals*, except for amber, coral, and pearl, which are organic in origin. The term *rock* generally refers to aggregates of minerals that have not been tampered with by humans. A *gemstone* is a mineral with certain physical properties that are valued by the jewelry trade, such as hardness, durability, and brilliance when cut. The term *crystal* is commonly used in referring to gemstones because of the geometrical symmetry of their internal structure. We will use the term *crystal* to specifically refer to clear quartz crystals. Finally, the word *stone* collectively refers to minerals, gemstones, or rocks. We will use these terms interchangeably, and the stones we have chosen are readily available, relatively inexpensive in their rough form, and ones we have personally found to be beneficial.

3

THE CRYSTAL OR THE GEMSTONE PATH?

When you are beginning to work with the Mineral Kingdom, it can be helpful to develop your sensitivity with one mineral. Broadening your knowledge of other stones will then be easier. Clear quartz crystal can be a good stone to begin with for this purpose. Its balanced structure and piezoelectric properties contribute to its qualities of versatility and amplification of intuitive communication skills. We consider it to be a "master teacher" of the mineral kingdom and have devoted *The Newcastle Guide to Healing with Crystals* to describing ways in which you can work with clear quartz.

However, it is also possible to begin work with a gemstone to which you feel attracted, using this book as a guide. Gemstones, because of their colors, are more specific in the range of their functions. Getting to know the gemstones is like meeting individual personalities, and helps to enrich your life through a wider experience of the Mineral Kingdom. If you are attracted to stones as a tool for spiritual gowth, you will probably be eager to become acquainted with both clear quartz and other gemstones as well. This book is devoted to describing a number of gemstones and ways in which you can work with clear quartz crystal to amplify your knowledge of other stones.

HARDNESS

There are a number of distinguishing characteristics that are used in identifying a gemstone. The first is *hardness*, its resistance to abrasion or scratching. The most common scale was developed by a Viennese mineralogist named Friedrich Mohs (1773–1839), who defined scratch hardness as the *resistance of a mineral when scratched with a pointed testing object*. Below, ten minerals are listed in their order of hardness on the Mohs' scale from 1 to 10, along with the Mohs' values of common items such as a fingernail and a copper coin.

By this scale a stone that remains unmarred after being scratched by a piece of window glass would have a hardness of more than 5½. In general, jewelry is made from gemstones that

Figure 1–1. The Mohs Scale of Hardness

1. talc
2. gypsum   (fingernail 2½)
3. calcite   (copper coin 3)
4. fluorite
5. apatite   (window glass 5½)

6. feldspar
7. quartz
8. topaz
9. corundum
10. diamond

test 7 or harder, because the softer minerals scratch more easily and are not as durable. Currently, the scratch hardness test has been largely abandoned in favor of optical testing methods for identifying gemstones. However, this test can still be useful if you simply want to know something about a rock that you pick up off the ground.

CHEMICAL COMPOSITION

Minerals can also be identified chemically. Most of the better known gems are mineral oxides or silicates. For example, all members of the quartz family, including clear quartz crystal, amethyst, and rose quartz, are silicon dioxide (SiO_2). Ruby and sapphire are aluminum oxide (Al_2O_3), and emerald, aquamarine, and beryl are aluminum beryllium silicate (Al_2Be_3(Si_6O_{18})). Oxides and silicates are often stable enough in their composition to resist decomposition, unlike sulphides and other mineral groupings. However, minerals with the same chemical composition can be quite different. Graphite and diamond are both carbon, but they are at opposite ends of the hardness scale because their crystalline structure is very different.

CRYSTALLINE STRUCTURE

Gemstones are highly structured, orderly lattices of molecules. The outer planes and surfaces of a stone can reflect the geometry of the internal structure. Most gemstones are not regularly shaped because some crystal faces are more pronounced, but the angle between the faces remains constant. Gemstones are classified into seven categories of crystalline structures, with varying degrees of symmetry. The explanation of the categories in Figures 1–2 through 1–8 comes from *The Spiritual Value of Gemstones* by Wallace G. Richardson and Lenora Huett.[1]

Note: The diagrams below will give a better visual presentation of the various basic crystal formations.

FIGURE 1–2. *The cubic system*, with three equal axes (a_1, a_2, a_3), arranged normal to each other:

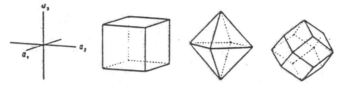

FIGURE 1–3. *The hexagonal system*, with four axes, three of which are arranged in one plane at 120° angles to each other. The main axis (c-axis) is normal to these three; it is an axis of sixfold symmetry:

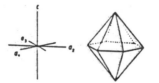

FIGURE 1–4. *The tetragonal system*, having two equal axes at 90° to each other (a_1 and a_2), and normal to these the main axis with fourfold symmetry:

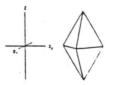

FIGURE 1–5. *The orthorhombic system*, with three unique axes (a, b, and c) at 90° to each other:

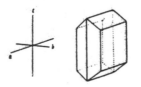

FIGURE 1–6. *The monoclinic system,* having three unequal axes (a, b, and c) at an obtuse angle to each other; b is normal to the plane formed by a and c:

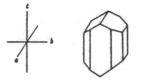

FIGURE 1–7. *The triclinic system,* having three axes of unequal length (a, b and c), all at obtuse angles to each other:

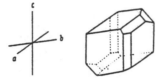

FIGURE 1–8. *The trigonal system,* using the same pattern as the hexogonal system. The main axis, however, has threefold symmetry only. This system is sometimes called the rhombohedral:

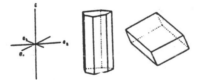

COLOR

One of the most fascinating aspects of gemstones is the way in which they absorb and reflect light. When light passes through a gemstone with no interruption, it is *transparent,* like clear quartz crystal. If a certain wave length of light is absorbed, the remaining mixture produces a color, and the gemstone is *translucent* or *opaque. Translucent* means allowing the passage of light but not primarily a clear view of any object. Moonstone and carnelian are examples of translucent stones. *Opaque* stones, such as blue lace agate and lapis lazuli, are impervious to light. If all the light is absorbed, then the stone appears black, as in black tourmaline. If all the wave lengths are absorbed in the same degree, the stone is a dull white or gray, as in white chalcedony.

Many gemstones, such as members of the quartz family, vary widely in color because of very small amounts of dispersed *impurities.* Clear quartz crystal becomes the deep violet of amethyst, due to minute traces of iron. Rose quartz gets its pink color from manganese or titanium. Other stones such as peridot and garnet are naturally colored without impurities.

Holes, bubbles, and irregularities in the crystalline structure are classified as *inclusions.* Inclusions can change the color, optical properties and mechanical resistance of a stone, and can also give certain stones their unique qualities. The play of colors in labradorite and opal are due to inclusions. During the formation of a corundum crystal, needlelike inclusions of rutile can form a hexagonal pattern which gives the effect of a six-rayed star in a cut stone. Such stones are known as star sapphires and star rubies.

The internal structures of a gemstone can act as a filter permitting certain kinds of light to pass through. Some gems will transmit different colors depending on the direction in which light passes through the stone. This phenomenon is called *pleochroism,* of which kunzite is an example. Kunzite can look lavender or pink, depending on which way you hold it to the light.

Color can also be altered by other effects. Clear quartz which has been exposed to radioactivity found at great underground depths absorbs ultraviolet light and becomes smoky quartz. Amethyst, rose quartz, and kunzite can become paler when exposed to direct sunlight over a period of time.

Some stones are heat-treated to change their colors. For example, amethyst is heated several hundred degrees to become reddish yellow citrine. In fact, many citrines are heat-treated amethyst. Other examples include dark green tourmalines heated to produce a lighter green. Practically all the deep blue aquamarine that is commonly available is heat-treated green or yellow beryl. Dealers are not required by law to state whether or not their stones have been heat-treated.

The color of a gem is further described according to its hue, tint, and intensity. Throughout history the most popular stones have been those with hues of red, green, or blue, dark rather than light tints, and high intensity. The darkest colored stones are cut thicker so that their color deepens.

OTHER PROPERTIES USED TO IDENTIFY GEMSTONES

There are several other properties used to identify gemstones. The first is *cleavage*, a term used to describe how gems split along certain flat planes. This property is related to their atomic structure. Stone setters must take the stone's cleavage into account, because if the stone is tapped too strongly or given too much pressure it will split along cleavage lines. Minerals that break easily are said to have perfect cleavage, and faceted gemstones with perfect cleavage indicate an artist's skill in handling them. Quartz does not break evenly or cleanly in any direction. In other words, it does not cleave. This lack of cleavage is a clue in identifying quartz. Some minerals such as calcite will cleave equally well in three directions, whereas topaz cleaves perfectly in only one direction. It is possible to see the cleavage planes by holding the stone and turning it slowly in the light. When the angle is right you can see the reflection of light from many small parallel and lustrous surfaces which are scattered at different levels along the break.

Another property is the *refractive index*. When you place a stick in water at a slant, the stick looks broken at the water level. This phenomenon is caused by the refraction of light as it leaves the air and enters obliquely into another substance such as water or a stone. The refractive angle is a reliable, useful tool in identifying gemstones.

Another useful tool is the *specific gravity* of a gem, or the expression of the relationship between the weight of a stone and the weight of an equal volume of water. Diamond is three and one-half times heavier than the same volume of water, so its specific gravity is 3½. The specific gravity of gems varies between 1 and 7. Values under 2 are light (amber is 1.1); those between 2 and 4 are normal (quartz is 2.6); and those above 4 are heavy (galena is 7.4).

Finally, gems are also identified by measuring their *absorption spectrum*, or the bands of color seen through a spectroscope. Each gem has a unique absorption spectrum consisting of broad bands of color interspersed with black vertical lines of differing widths. The absorption spectrum can be used to distinguish between imitation, synthetic, and natural stones. We will discuss this later.

CUTTING AND POLISHING

There are three basic operations in preparing a gemstone from the rough: sawing, grinding, and polishing. The cutting of colored stones is called *lapidary work*, and the cutter is a *lapidary*. A stone is first sawed into shape with a rotating disk of iron or bronze that is impregnated with diamond powder. The coolant is soapy water, oil, or paraffin. The final shape is cut on a vertical, roughly grained carborundum wheel and cooled with water.

In general there are three different types of cut: the *facet*, the *plain cut*, and the *mixed cut*. The facet cut is applied to transparent stones because the small even facets give the gem a higher luster and a better play of color. Most facet cuts are built on two basic types. The *brilliant cut*, with thirty-two or more facets, is used with diamonds and other stones with a high refractive index, to bring out their brilliance. The *emerald*, or *step cut*, features a large central rectangular facet called a *table facet*, which gives a good view of the color of the stone. The faceting of stones is a specialized art first developed around the fifteenth century, and is enjoyed today by hobbyists as well as professionals.

The *plain cut* is a much simpler process than faceting and is used for agates, opaque stones, and stones with inclusions. The bottom is cut level and the top is either level or, more often, domed. A stone with a domed or rounded top is called a *cabochon* (cab' a shawn). In a *mixed cut* the upper part is level and the lower part is faceted.

GEM SUBSTITUTES

These stones are classified as imitations, reconstructed stones, or synthetic stones. *Imitation* stones originated with the

Egyptians and are usually made today with glass or plastic. *Reconstructed* stones are made by fusing a piece of natural stone to another piece of artificial material such as glass or foil. For example, a "triplet" is made by fusing two layers of a natural gemstone with colored glue between them, like a sandwich. An example of a "doublet" would be a colorless beryl crown cemented to a piece of green glass to produce a stone that looks like an emerald. The joint of an assembled or reconstructed stone is often covered by the setting, but will show under magnification. Dyes and plastics are commonly used to impregnate porous gems such as turquoise to make them brighter and more durable.

Synthetic gemstones are identical chemically and structurally to their natural counterparts. They are made by a flame fusion process in which powdered raw material is melted in a furnace at 1360 degrees fahrenheit. The molten drops fall onto a cradle, where they crystallize and form a pearshaped "boule." The gems are then cut from these boules.

The reason gemstones are altered is to make less expensive jewelry. All gems with artificial changes, except for heat-treated stones and dyed agates, must be marked as such when offered for sale. It is wise to check with the dealer to make sure you are getting exactly what you want.

TYPES OF DEPOSITS AND MINING

In order to find the natural stones, it helps to know a little about rock formation. There are three major types of rock formations in the Earth: *igneous, sedimentary,* and *metamorphic.* Igneous rocks are the solidification of magma or molten rock over a period of time. Plutonic igneous rocks such as granite and quartz are formed deep below the Earth's surface. Due to their long process of formation, the individual crystals have sufficient time to grow quite large. Volcanic igneous rocks such as obsidian are formed directly from molten rocks that have cooled near the earth's surface, and are without a visible crystalline structure.

Igneous rocks are generally harder than 5½, with a crystalline texture of interlocking mineral grains. In general, light-colored igneous rocks are rich in the light-colored minerals: quartz, alkali feldspars, and muscovite mica. Chemically these rocks have an excess of silica. Dark-colored igneous rocks lack silica, but are rich in iron- and magnesium-bearing minerals, and in the calcium and sodium feldspars. The most common rock-forming minerals are quartz and feldspars.

Many gem minerals are found in *pegmatites*, which are lens-like bodies of more coarsely grained igneous rocks that cut across the finer-grained parent rock. Pegmatites were originally cavities containing gas and residual fluids escaping from the cooling granite magma. These cavities were like wombs in which crystalline structures of various kinds formed over a period of time under high pressure and temperature. Pegmatites therefore are excellent sites for mineral and gemstone collecting.

Sedimentary rocks are formed under moderate pressure from layers of accumulated sediment and deposits of organic matter. Sedimentary rocks tend to be layered, and fossils are commonly found in them. Sandstone and limestone are examples of sedimentary rocks. Sometimes the harder gemstones will be found in the softer sedimentary host rock that has begun to wear away.

Metamorphic rocks are already existing igneous or sedimentary rocks that are subjected to chemical activity, heat, or pressure, which reorganizes their mineral composition. They essentially undergo changes without becoming fluid and are often conspicuously bent or folded. Schist and gneiss are examples of metamorphic rocks. Knowing something about the host rocks can help you know where to look for gemstones.

MINERAL FAMILIES

A number of gemstones are actually varieties of quartz, feldspar, and other mineral groupings. We will now describe the relevant groupings so that you will understand some similarities in the physical properties of the stones in each grouping.

Quartz, or silicon dioxide, accounts for about twelve percent of the earth's crust, and can be found in igneous, sedimentary, and metamorphic rocks. The hardness of quartz and its chemical stability under weathering make it the last residue of a great variety of rocks. We can divide the quartz family into several groupings:

1. *Macrocrystalline quartz* grows in veins or cavities that are partially filled with silica. Under favorable conditions in pegmatite, crystals of clear, smoky, or amethyst quartz can grow to several hundred pounds. This group of quartz, with the exception of rose quartz, is commonly found in the familiar form of six sides and a termination point. These quartzes are named according to their color:
   a. Amethyst: pale violet to deep purple
   b. Clear quartz: sometimes called rock crystal, clear
   c. Citrine: clear yellow, golden yellow
   d. Smoky quartz: smoky or grayish brown to black
   e. Rose quartz: pink
   f. Black tourmalinated quartz: clear quartz with inclusions of black tourmaline
   g. Rutiliated quartz: clear or smoky quartz with needle-like inclusions of rutile

2. In the chalcedony or *microcrystalline* quartz group, the silica forms compact masses of tiny crystals which are dull rather than glassy in appearance. Generally microcrystalline quartz is formed near the surface of the Earth, where temperatures and pressures are relatively lower. Here are the microcrystalline quartzes that are included in this book:
   a. Aventurine: quartz colored with iridescent green mica
   b. Chalcedony: white, blue or gray (We describe the white chalcedony in this book.)
   c. Chrysoprase: opaque apple green
   d. Bloodstone: opaque dark green with spots of red jasper (also called heliotrope)

e.   Carnelian: translucent red, orange, or yellow

f.   Moss agate: translucent milky white with moss-like green incusions of hornblende

g.   Tiger's Eye: gold-yellow to gold-brown layers

2.   The *agates* are quartzes of the microcrystalline type which have a concentric banded structure. Agates are usually found in volcanic rocks. Sometimes they are stained chemically to make their colors brighter:

a.   Blue lace agate: light blue and white layers

b.   Fire agate: various shades of brown layers

The *feldspar* make up the largest group of minerals and are found in all volcanic rocks. The colors in granite come from its feldspar content. Feldspars are slightly softer than quartz, registering about 6 on the Mohs' scale. There are sub-groupings of feldspars, based on cleavage and chemical composition, depending on whether they are potassium aluminum silicates or sodium calcium silicates. This book includes:

1.   Amazonite: opaque blue-green, light turquoise (sometimes called amazon stone)

2.   Moonstone: colorless or milky to faintly yellow, will show a silvery blue sheen in reflected light

3.   Labradorite: gray with brilliant iridescent colors at certain angles in reflected ight

4.   Orange sunstone: red-orange or red-brown with metallic glitter (sometimes called aventurine feldspar)

5.   Yellow orthoclase feldspar: translucent yellow (sometimes called yellow sunstone).

Corundum is normally found in a type of marble formed from limestone which has been subjected to metamorphic action. Corundum has a Mohs' standard of 9 and is prized for its hard durability and brilliant colors when faceted. We include:

1.   Ruby: red

2.   Sapphire: colors other than red, such as blue and clear.

The *beryl* gemstones, with a hardness of 7½–8, are among the most widely known and differ in color only, due to the presence of trace elements. We include:

1.   Emerald: rich green

2.   Aquamarine: light blue, light blue-green.

2 | Spiritual Aspects of Gemstones

IF YOU ARE READING this book you may already have been to your local rock shop and stood in awe of the beautiful colors and patterns in the stones. It is possible you enjoy the smooth solidity of a beach pebble and the way it connects you with the Earth. Whatever path you are traveling, you may have decided that it is now time to reconnect with the Earth and to experience its wisdom at deeper levels.

In order to understand the wisdom of stones, you need to begin to perceive all life as different frequencies and forms of *energy*. This energy can be experienced at the physical, emotional, mental, and spiritual levels. In this chapter we will review the concept of life-force energy and the human energy system. We will then become more attuned to the Spiritual Levels of Reality, where life-force energy creates and balances our natural physical world. We will talk about how our individual journeys to discover the meaning of life influence our perceptions of the life-force energies in gemstones. Finally, we will describe how you can choose and care for your gemstones.

REVIEWING LIFE-FORCE ENERGY AND THE HUMAN ENERGY SYSTEM

Everything in Nature consists of life-force energy vibrating at different levels. On the physical level, life-force energy ultimately becomes matter. On the spiritual level, life-force energy is Consciousness expressed as qualities such as courage, joy, and compassion. Life-force energy is known to have healing qualities, and it is these spiritual healing qualities which we seek in the stones. Your thoughts also have varying amounts of life-force energy, depending on how positive they are. When you combine the life-force energy in conscious positive thoughts or affirmations with the life-force energy of the stones, the healing potential is greater than the energy of either the thoughts or stones separately.

Your body is a complex energy system. The *aura* or energy field surrounding your body is composed of several layers or *subtle bodies.* Our working system roughly defines three layers, which correspond to the physical, emotional-mental, and spiritual levels of development. We combine the emotional and mental levels together, as they both influence the creation of conscious beliefs.

The physical layer is usually called the *etheric body* and extends out about one-quarter inch to two or three inches from the physical body. Being the densest layer, it is the easiest to perceive and is sometimes seen as a thin band of white or grayish light. When you wear or place stones on your body you are directly affecting the etheric body, which serves as a blueprint for the physical body.

Surrounding the etheric body are the *emotional and mental* subtle bodies. We sense these layers from three or four inches to about twelve inches above the body. These fields are often seen clairvoyantly as shimmering, changing colors that indicate the emotional and mental state of a person's thoughts.

The *spiritual subtle body* extends from about twelve inches to two or three feet from the physical body. This is the level where you merge with your Higher Self and are connected with the reality beyond your conscious awareness.

Your subtle bodies are highly sensitive to thought forms. When a thought form enters one of your subtle bodies, the structure of that body changes to resonate with the thought. Depending on the nature of the thought, the subtle body either becomes more stable, structured, and filled with life-force energy, or more disorganized. This process happens quickly and spontaneously with your passing thoughts. That is why clairvoyants often see many colors, including predominant overtones, as well as various changing colors. Your very being is structured by thoughts. Therefore, you can use positive thoughts to affect your sensitive energy fields to bring about balance.

In addition to serving as both a blueprint for the body and a record of your experiences, the subtle bodies also serve as transducers of life-force energy. As you receive life-force energy from a variety of sources, including thought, it is stepped down at each level and made into a grosser or denser form that your body can use.

The *chakras* form another component of your energy system. The chakras are energy vortexes, or "wheels of light," which both connect the subtle bodies and act as transducers for life-force energy. There are seven major chakras, associated with the major endocrine glands. The chakras represent physical, emotional, mental, and spiritual levels of development. As you evolve in understanding both your interdependence with others as well as the Oneness of All Life, your chakras receive more life-force energies at increasingly finer frequencies. The levels of development represented by each chakra, and their locations on the human body, are summarized in Figures 3–1 and 3–2 at the end of Chapter 3.

The thymus gland, a less understood component of the human energy system, receives and directs life-force energies. It is located in the middle of the chest between the breasts and the hollow of the throat (See figure 3–1). The thymus gland was originally thought to have no function at all because it seems to atrophy in many people after the age of thirteen. It is not generally known that the thymus gland shrinks during serious illness and severe physical stress.

The thymus gland is more clearly understood in terms of its

spiritual function. It is a very sensitive gland and is activated by *positive mental attitudes*. Apparently, it remains largely dormant unless you consciously practice giving and receiving Unconditional Love, with the realization that your thoughts affect your body. However, once you welcome Unconditional Love in the form of positive thoughts and spiritual understanding into your life, the thymus gland is activated to do two things. First, it acts as a sensor that detects where an imbalance of life-force energy is occurring in the body. Second, apparently it can transduce the life-force energy of thought and direct it for rebalancing the physical body. Thus, it monitors and regulates the body's immune system when the mind-body connection is understood. The thymus gland is discussed again in Chapter 7.

The energy system of the body reflects the electromagnetic properties of life-force energy. One side of the body and one hand carry a negative electrical charge and a north pole magnetic charge. In this book, we call the negative hand the *receiving hand*. The other side of the body and the opposite hand carry a positive charge and a south pole magnetic charge. We call the positive hand the *sending hand*. To determine your sending and receiving hands, you will need two single-pointed clear quartz crystals:

1. Place one crystal in your hand, with the point facing toward your body, and the other in your opposite hand, with the point toward your fingertips. Be aware of how your energy is moving in your body. Is there a flow?

2. Now point each crystal in the opposite direction, reversing the circuit. Check your energy again. Is there a flow now?

One circuit will often feel more open than the other. The hand in which the crystal points toward the body becomes your *receiving hand* and the hand in which the crystal points away from your body becomes your *sending hand*. When you wish to receive energy from a stone or meditate with it, hold it in your receiving hand. If you want to work with others, hold the stone in your sending hand.

Either your receiving hand or your sending hand can be your *sensing hand.* To determine your sensing hand you will need a single crystal:

1. Hold your hands about four inches apart, as if you were holding an imaginary ball, with the crystal in your right hand. The point is facing the left palm.

2. Draw circles in the field in front of the left palm.

3. Repeat with the crystal in the left hand pointing toward the right palm.

The sensations will be stronger and more pronounced in your *sensing* hand. Hold a stone in your sensing hand when you want to understand its energy or to check if it needs cleaning or charging. You also work with your sensing hand to check the energy field surrounding the body of someone your are working on.

THE SPIRITUAL REALITY OF THE DEVIC KINGDOMS OF NATURE

Just as you learn to perceive life-force energy in your own system, you can learn to perceive life-force energy in the Kingdoms of Nature. All of Nature exists in physical forms that you experience with your five senses, as well as in Spiritual Forms, which are part of the larger reality. The Kingdoms of Nature can teach you about the Spiritual Dimensions of physical reality and the Divine Source that is present in all life.

Just as you have a Higher Self that is able to share universal wisdom and guide you in ways that you can understand, each mineral also has a "Higher Self" called a *Deva.* The information that follows is channeled from a Clear Quartz Crystal Deva, which is one level of Deva that works with a particular species or form:

"Let me tell you some things about myself and the Devic Kingdom. My Kingdom is based in the world of Spirit. We are Light Beings with light bodies that are essentially formless, although we are capable of taking on form. Our Will is the Will of the Divine and we communicate directly with the Divine Source. That is the same as your being with your Higher Self.

"Everything consists of life-force energy. As a Crystal Deva one of my purposes is to create a blueprint for the physical crystal form from life-force energy. I am like an architect, working with the material of life-force energy to create a unique form. I am also like a manager in that I work with the life-force energies to maintain an ongoing, optimal balance in the crystals I work with. This balance is always changing, as the crystals give and receive according to their own needs, and I keep the life-force energies flowing in a stabilized manner."

Another level of Devas we call Overlighting Devas. Their purpose is to maintain a stable flow and balance of life-force energies in a geographical area or among groups of forms. The Overlighting Deva of the Mineral Kingdom talks with us about what we can learn from the Kingdom of Nature:

"First of all, you need to work co-creatively with Nature in order to survive. We do not see the Kingdoms of Nature as separate from the Human Kingdom as you do. We see the connectedness and interdependence of all life and we wish to share this message with you in as many ways as we can. The process of maintaining balance for Planet Earth emphasizes interdependence. You cannot live without the energy received from the Sun, which the Plant Kingdom gives to you in a usable form. The life that a life form releases as a gift of service is a growth enhancer for another Kingdom. You can learn about any Kingdom of Nature by linking your being with it.

"It is important for you to see yourselves as a positive part of the balancing process of the Planet. Plants, animals, and minerals willingly give their life-force energies for your rebalancing. Whenever you are ''drawn'' to a certain stone, your Higher Self is telling you that you can benefit from the qualities of that stone. You need only listen to your intuitive guidance. As you better understand how to heal your sickness with your thoughts and the healing energies of Nature, you will strengthen the vitality of the entire planet.

''All of life operates first at a very dense level of matter and at very specific frequencies, and continues to evolve until it reaches the stage where it can work creatively with broad frequencies of formless energy. In this evolutionary cycle the Human Kingdom is not the highest form of life. You are learning to bring your own will into union with the Divine Will. You are learning to focus both your emotional being and your thoughts in order to bring about what you are seeking. When your will is in harmony with Divine Will you can move into the Spiritual Realm, where you work with your creative capacities in Oneness with the Universal.

''We Devas can share with you from our perspective of the Universal Oneness. Whenever you seek to learn from any member of the Mineral Kingdom, you need to release all sense of judgment as it relates to us or to the wisdom that we share. Communication becomes difficult when you approach us with the sense that you are truly the all-knowledgeable ones. You ask why we wait for the Human Kingdom to initiate contact with us. The answer is that for us to contact you requires an expenditure of life-force energies that we prefer to direct in balancing and harmonizing the planet's life-force energies. You must use your will to seek contact with us.

''You must also learn to release self-judgment and exercise the qualities of acceptance and patience as they relate to the communication that you receive from us. Each time that you seek to enter our dimensionless space and are harboring judgment about your ability to receive, at the moment in time you have blocked the path for communication to take place. We are aware of when you are in the space of internal struggle and doubt, whether it relates to us or the material that is being shared. I say, trust that the process of learning is evolving and becoming more pure. Each time we come together, we harmonize the energies between your Kingdom and mine.

"One of our functions is to step down life-force energies from the Masters and from other levels of reality into forms that you humans can understand and work with in your thoughts and in your physical bodies. Your physical world serves as an embodiment of Spiritual Truths that you perceive with your five senses and your human form. The Kingdoms of Nature teach you not only to see with physical eyes, but to expand in your awareness beyond the limitations of physical form. We Devas are therefore a Light Bridge for you to understand your Oneness. Be open to the Light that the Kingdoms of Nature have to share with you. We of the Devic Kingdom give our service to you joyfully. Feel the peace of our presence."

Here are some ways you can begin to attune to the Devic Kingdom through your gemstones:

1. Holding your gemstones, breathe deeply, relax your body, and mentally go to a natural place where you feel safe and totally at peace. Affirm that your Higher Self is with you and remain receptive for a few minutes.

2. Now focus your awareness on the gemstone in your hand. Thank the God/Goddess/All That Is for Its being and express your gratitude for the gifts of the Earth.

3. Look upon your stone with humility and respect, as a friend who can teach you and help you. Affirm that the Deva of your stone is now with you and wait receptively. See if you can notice the energy shift from your Higher Self to the Deva. You may feel a sense of calm joy, or perhaps another energy sensation, such as a specific visual pattern of colors.

In your mind you can repeat the process by first calling your Higher Self and then the Deva, so that you can clarify the energy differences in your being.

4. Ask the Deva to share the guidance you need from the stone and allow yourself to receive it. If you would like to clarify what you receive, you can ask yes/no questions using the pendulum. You might ask, "Are you helping to restore physical vitality to my body?" or "Am I to carry you with me?"

5. Thank the Deva and the stone for their help and love. Every stone has a gift to offer the Human Kingdom. You merely need to be patient and persistent in learning to adjust your spiritual energy to that of the stone. The Devas very much wish to work with us; it is primarily a matter of establishing an "open line" and an intuitive language. Once you have linked with the stone on a spiritual level, you do not always need to be in an altered state of consciousness to consciously receive from the stone. As you deepen your spiritual awareness you will find that you receive from the stone in your own unique ways.

THE INFLUENCE OF BELIEFS UPON OUR PERCEPTIONS OF GEMSTONE QUALITIES

When you sense the non-physical properties of a stone, your conscious beliefs have a direct impact on what you perceive. As humans we have a range of skills and abilities related to our purpose in life. Each of us in our unique way has the opportunity to serve in the overall balance. Stones also have a range of qualities or attributes related to their purpose in being and the service that they give. They have both a physical and a spiritual purpose. Physically they are a foundation for all of life. Spiritually each stone is an expression of Consciousness or Love, and exists in complete Oneness with All That Is. However, the manner in which we humans experience this Oneness differs according to our individual religious and cultural training.

When you work with stones, you interpret their Conscious-

ness according to your own spiritual understanding. You tend toward consistency in your belief systems and consequently, you do one of two things: either you interpret your perceptions in a manner consistent with other things that you know and understand, or you dismiss the perception from your conscious mind. In the past the spiritual qualities of stones were not understood and were dismissed as "magic."

Your beliefs affect your perception of events. For example, many of you who never noticed "coincidences" before may later come to realize that they are guidance from your intuition. Then you begin to notice lots of coincidences that were actually happening all along, without your awareness. In this way you become aware of how your beliefs create your reality.

Your relationships with stones and all the Kingdoms of Nature is an interdependent one. You relate to the stones according to your purpose in being. Those of you who are involved in helping others heal their physical bodies may relate to stones according to their physical healing properties. Those who work with emotional and spiritual healing may relate to the spiritual healing aspects of the stones. You understand the stones according to how you perceive them as helping you fulfill your purpose.

Your physical and emotional well-being affects your sensitivity to the stones. If your body is out of balance from drugs, alcholol, or stimulants, or your emotions are in a state of imbalance, you will be less sensitive to the energies of the stones. Once you undertake a program of physical well-being, not only is it easier for you to sense the qualities of gemstones, but you can allow them to work to their maximum energy potential. Physical well-being includes a healthy diet, exercise, the cleansing of toxins, and an emotionally nurturing environment.

Your "body constitution" also influences how you perceive gemstone energy. Someone who is very physically active, with an outgoing, expressive nature, may feel an active, energetic stone like ruby to be balancing and maybe even soothing. Someone else, with a quieter, gentler, less active constitution, might find ruby highly stimulating and may find that rose quartz feels more balancing.

When you look at a stone your first perceptions may be related to its color. Therefore, you interpret its energy according to your experiences with color. For example, I relate to orange as a stimulating color and tend to experience orange carnelian as a dynamic stone. Jonathan relates to orange in terms of warmth and often experiences orange carnelian as a warm, gently expanding stone.

The way in which you move through the lessons of your life affects your perceptions. Once in a workshop we had two people describe their experiences with malachite. One peson was not happy with it at all and could not wait to put it down. A second woman was quite comfortable with malachite and had a sense that she needed to hold onto it. Our experience with malachite is that it has an intense quality which can rapidly focus your awareness on fear that you need to release. The first person was not in a place to look at emotional change at that time. She enjoyed and needed the stones at the workshop that felt gentle and grounding to her. The second woman was very comfortable with the intensity of malachite and was in the middle of an emotional transition. You are drawn to the stones that are best for you at any given time.

GEMSTONE CORRELATIONS: ASTROLOGY AND OTHER METAPHYSICAL BELIEF SYSTEMS

There are many different associations that people have made between gemstones, the planets, and the signs of the zodiac. The planets and stars, like everything else in nature, have spiritual qualities to which you are particularly receptive at the time of your birth. Your astrological natal chart is a descrption of how the qualities of the planets and signs of the zodiac are interwoven to help shape both your outer and inner natures. The spiritual qualities of the planets and signs are perceived intuitively and therefore are related to the beliefs and experiences of the person describing them. The associations of gemstones with signs and planets are thus subjective and individual and based on linking similar qualities according to a certain perceptual framework.

If you are already attuned to the system of astrology, or for that matter, numerology, tarot, or the Kabbalah, you can use the elements of your system to understand the healing qualities of the stones. As you merge your system with the use of stones, you will attain a broader knowledge of the stones and find new ways to work them into your system.

It is important to remember that there are many reasons why descriptions of gemstone qualities are so different. You should honor the varying experiences you share with each other. It is best to form your own relationships with the stones and trust your perceptions and beliefs. *Understand that what you read is truth for the person or persons who wrote it and that you are in the process of expanding your own truth. At all times honor and learn from your own perceptions.*

CHOOSING GEMSTONES

When you go to purchase gemstones you will find them offered in three major forms: *rough, polished* or *tumbled,* and *faceted.* Each form has its advantages and disadvantages and it is entirely a matter of personal preference which form you choose. Rough stones found at gem shows and lapidary shops are large in size, unshaped by humans, and quite inexpensive. Polished stones, also found at gem shows and rock shops, come in two shapes. The cabochons are often oval, flat on the bottom, and domed on top. Polished or tumbled stones, which are more rounded, have been shaped in machines called tumblers. The stone is placed in water in the tumbler along with finer and finer grades of grit, while the tumbler motor agitates the stone. Polished stones show the intricate nuances of the colors within them better than rough stones and are also inexpensive. Faceted stones, found at gem shows and jewelry stores, are cut to reflect light and their colors are usually brilliant and clear. They are much more expensive than either rough or polished stones.

You have to decide how you personally feel about stones that have been shaped by humans. Lapidaries who work with an eye only on profit will add a different energy to the stone than those who work with an attitude of honor and love. A great deal of stone is "wasted" in the cutting process and discarded. On the other hand, a skilled artist with love and knowledge of the stone can create a true gift of beauty and service. Ultimately the energy of a gemstone is a blend of your beliefs, your love for the stone, and the energy of the stone itself, as well as the energy of those who have been significantly involved in it.

In choosing gemstones, try to be guided by your intuition as much as possible. If you ask for the appropriate guidance Nature will always guide you to what you need. When you are attracted to the color of a particular stone, or you keep thinking about it after seeing it, your intuition is probably telling you that you can benefit from the qualities of that stone. When you are choosing a stone, relax, breathe deeply, and put yourself in touch with a sense of reverence and gratitude. In this way you will be open and receptive for guidance to come to you.

CARING FOR GEMSTONES

Gemstones, like clear quartz crystals, need to be cleared and charged. Once you have chosen your gemstones and brought them home, it is wise first to clear them of imbalanced vibrations picked up from handling by others. As you charge the stones they begin to attune to your energies because you are involved in the process. If the desire to immediately start carrying your stones with you is overwhelming (as it sometimes is!) you can always buy two stones of the same kind and clean and charge one and carry the other.

There are a number of practices for clearing and charging given in *The Newcastle Guide to Healing with Crystals* which we will not repeat here. You can decide intuitively with either a pendulum or through inner sensing which methods are best for you.

A common practice for clearing your gemstones is to soak them in a solution of sea salt and spring water, both of which you can buy at the grocery store. We have used anywhere from one-half teaspoon to one-quarter cup of salt to two cups of water. The clearing process seems to take longer for gemstones than for clear quartz crystals. We have soaked our gemstones from overnight to as long as three weeks. If we choose this method, we check the stones daily with a pendulum to see if they are adequately cleared. We have also learned through practice with the pendulum how to tell by simply holding them if they are clear. When clear, a stone has a neutral, empty feeling. Generally, several days is a useful rule of thumb. We have also discovered that the more sensitive we become to gemstone energies the more often we clean them, because the difference in their effectiveness is dramatically apparent.

A method we have used in the past to charge the stones is to place them in sunlight or under a pyramid for approximately six hours. A charged stone gives off a dynamic, "electric" quality that you can usually feel in various parts of your body. The more a stone loses its charge, the less you will feel its energy in your body. We like to have more than one piece of a particular gemstone, so that we have one to work with while the others are clearing and charging.

Your beliefs affect the manner in which the stones receive energy when charging. For example, if you believe that the stones will receive less energy if you leave them outside on a cloudy night, that is indeed what will happen.

As we have learned how to work with the Devas, we have come to better understand how much they can help us in healing co-creatively. Currently we clear and charge our gemstones in the following manner:

1. Place the stone or stones to be cleared in a bowl of water.

2. Become still within and merge with the beauty and healing energy in the stones and in All Creation. Allow yourself to receive the healing energy.

3. Ask the Devas to help in clearing the stones, keeping your mind focused on a visualization of the stones being cleared. For example, you can visualize them pure and clear in the sunlight.

4. Ask the Devas to help in charging the stones, keeping your mind focused on the stones being filled with your breath, sunlight, Unconditional Love, and Vitality.

5. After a couple of minutes, or when you sense that the process has ended, thank the Devas for their help and, if possible, leave the bowl outside for three hours or so. If you need the stones cleared and charged in a shorter time, be specific about the time period.

If you remember to see both the clearing and charging as a learning process, you will be able to develop your most effective personal methods.

3 | Learning About Gem Energy: Color, Sound, and Chakra Affinities

Iɴ ᴛʜɪs ᴄʜᴀᴘᴛᴇʀ we will begin the process of experiencing the spiritual qualities of gemstones by observing them from several perspectives: color, sound, and chakra and subtle body affinities. By perceiving gemstone qualities through different perceptual frameworks, you can increase your understanding of their versatility. You also sharpen your own intuitive skills and find which perspectives are most natural to you.

Life-force energies can be perceived through the mediums of color and sound. We will first discuss correspondences of gemstone energy and the spiritual qualities of colors. Our second perspective in learning about gem energy is sound. By sensitizing yourself to sound, you can learn to find a stone's dominant frequency, or *soul tone*. The soul tone, like a stone's color, is a key to understanding its spiritual qualities and the particular gifts it has to offer.

Our third perspective in learning about gem energy involves learning to sense a stone's affinities for various chakras and subtle bodies. Each stone has an individual purpose or gift to give, just as each of us has a particular purpose in being. For this reason each stone will show an affinity for particular chakras and subtle bodies in your energy field.

PERSPECTIVE ONE—COLOR

We have previously stated that life-force energy has physical, emotional, mental, and spiritual qualities which are expressed by all living things, including gemstones. We can further state that color and sound are defined in physical terms as different expressions of the same healing life-force energy. On the spiritual level it is possible to sense color as sound and sound as color. Let us now look at color as a way of understanding the qualities of gemstones.

All light is visible radiant energy which travels through space in the form of waves. It travels 186,000 miles per second in varying wavelengths. At the cosmic end of the scale, wavelengths are so short that millions of waves placed end to end will fit within an area the size of a postage stamp. At the opposite end of the spectrum the largest waves may exceed one hundred thousand miles in length. Located near the middle of the spectrum is the tiny band of radiant energy which is visible to the human eye—the color spectrum.

In Indian philosophy the spiritual qualities of color are closely linked to the seven major chakras; this is the system we work with.

Red

Red, associated with the root chakra, is an intense, focused vibration that builds vitality on the physical level. On the emotional and mental levels, red gives courage and perseverance. On the spiritual level red strengthens the will and helps you affirm your basic existence as a unique individual.

Affirmation: "With red I move forward in life with courage and confidence."

Orange

Orange, associated with the lower abdomen chakra, is a warm, expansive vibration that energizes on the physical level.

On the emotional and mental levels orange stimulates optimism and hope, which makes it a good antidote for fear and depression. On the spiritual level its expansive quality encourages you to broaden your experience in order to expand who you are.

Affirmation: "With orange I expand my optimism and faith."

Yellow

Yellow, associated with the solar plexus chakra, is a light, stimulating vibration on the physical level. On the emotional and mental levels its sunny qualities include joy, optimism, and confidence. Yellow expands your understanding by fine-tuning your decision-making mind and uplifting you to broader perspectives. It is associated with problem-solving, inventiveness, and, on the spiritual level, joy in being alive.

Affirmation: "With yellow I bring joy, mental clarity, and confidence to all that I do."

Green

Green is associated with the heart chakra and has an affinity with the physical body and the earth. Physically, it is soothing and balancing. On the emotional and mental levels green encourages the resolution of conflict through compassion and self-acceptance. Green is also associated with gratitude and material expansion, perhaps because green is the predominant color of the abundance of Nature. Spiritually, green encourages you to trust in the process of growth.

Affirmation: "With green I flow with emotional balance and harmony."

Blue

Blue is associated with the throat chakra and, like green, is physically calming and relaxing. On the emotional and mental levels blue gives qualities of idealism, devotion, and understanding as you begin to express your purpose and aspirations in life.

On the spiritual level blue can add perspective to your experience through its elevating and peaceful qualities.

Affirmation: "With blue I am steady, calm, and at peace."

Indigo

Indigo, associated with the third eye chakra, is a deep blue tinged with violet, like the color of the twilight sky. Indigo is a very light, cooling vibration attuned to the spiritual subtle body. Indigo gives an expanded understanding of your everyday world by lifting you into the world of spirit.

Affirmation: "With indigo my inner sensitivity to all life expands and becomes clearer."

Violet

Violet, associated with the crown chakra, is even lighter, cooler, and more subtle. Spiritually, it helps you transcend and transform your experience so that you feel a sense of Unity with All. It stimulates qualities of truth, devotion, and responsibility. Violet also helps you let go of beliefs that keep you feeling separated from others.

Affirmation: "With violet, I go beyond my personal existence to become a part of All That Is."

Pink

Pink works particularly well with the emotional and spiritual subtle bodies and is often associated with the heart chakra. It has a lighter vibration than green and gives qualities of delight, compassion, playfulness, and self-acceptance.

Affirmation: "With pink, I enjoy being who I am."

It is important to develop your own intuitive sense of the colors and their qualities. Here are several ways that you can do this:

1. Focus your awareness on the colors in your daily life. The colors of your clothing can have a healing effect if you take

time to merge with them and affirm their qualities. You can choose clothing intuitively on the basis of what you need.

2. When you want to understand how you really feel about something, use oil pastels, water colors, magic markers, etc., and draw in color. Let yourself express freely on paper, and then go back and notice what colors you used. You will learn a lot about how you relate personally to colors.

3. Work with visualizations in color. When you wish to relax, visualize the woods or the meadow in as much color detail as you can. Visualize sunsets and sunrises, or make up your fantasies in Technicolor. Visualizing colors in your mind helps strengthen your subconscious attunement to color.

4. Work with color meditations.

   a. Inhale while visualizing red expanding from your diaphragm. Hold your breath briefly and focus on red, then slowly exhale red throughout your body. Continue through the rest of the spectrum, breathing three or more times for each color. You can pause after each color and be aware of how each color affects you.

   b. Do a chakra color meditation, breathing red into your root chakra, orange into your lower abdomen, and so on through the color spectrum.

   c. An interesting variation is to choose one chakra, particularly a chakra in which you tend to block energy, and breathe each color into that chakra. Notice which colors seem to affect this chakra.

   d. Another system you might use in breathing color into the chakras comes from Bernard Gunther's *Energy Ecstasy*.[1] This system gives some other interesting insights into the relationship of color and the chakras which we found useful in understanding chakra placements for gemstones:

root chakra	red-orange
lower abdomen chakra	pink
solar plexus chakra	kelly green
heart chakra	yellow-gold

throat chakra	sky blue
third eye chakra	indigo
crown chakra	purple

It is important to note here that at times each chakra will benefit from a variety of colors. The color associated with a chakra has certain qualities that are relevant to the developmental issues of that chakra. When working intuitively with color, be open to giving any area of your body whatever color it needs. You will broaden your understanding of color and gemstones as well.

Now you are ready to work with the gemstones:

1. If possible, have a friend place a gemstone in your hand without your looking at it.

2. Try to sense what you are experiencing on all levels. Observe your perceptions.

3. Then look at the stone, sense it again, and be aware of any added perceptions that you receive from the color. How did seeing the color affect your perceptions of the stone?

Understanding the gemstone qualities in terms of color is a good starting place. However, this perspective can be incomplete by itself. We were given guidance to try some other perspectives, the next of which is sound.

PERSPECTIVE TWO—SOUND

Sound, as well as color, can express qualities on the physical, emotional, mental, and spiritual levels. It takes practice to become sensitive to sound within your body. However, once you are more intuitively sensitive to sound, it becomes another medium through which you can better understand the properties of gemstones. Sound is also a powerful tool for healing.

Toning is the practice of making sounds with your voice for healing. To label particular tones, you can use a pitch pipe or a musical instrument. To loosen up your voice and get acquainted with making sounds and tones, try the following exercises:

1. This first clearing exercise can be done anywhere and is good for the release of physical and emotional tension. Begin as low as you can go and make a sound like a siren, that moves up the scale as high as you can go, and back down again. Do this several times and notice the reaction in your body. Do you feel a little lighter and more free?

2. Try making different tones and sounds and see which ones you like and which tones resonate or reverberate inside you. You might find yourself focusing on one tone, or making up a little tune. Notice whether your body feels more charged. You are making an intuitive connection with sound.

A step that is relevant to working with gemstones is to sense the resonance between sound and color. Clear quartz crystal can be an invaluable aid as an amplifier in this process. To establish your own connections between sound and color as well as how the resonance feels in your body, try the following exercise:

1. Hold a clear quartz crystal in your sending hand with the point facing away from your body.

2. Tone a middle C through the crystal as if it were a microphone. While you are toning middle C, visualize the color red as vividly as you can, being aware of what is happening in your body.

3. Now tone a different note, such as A, while still visualizing red, and discriminate the differences in your body. You are looking for what gives you a greater energy stimulation.

However, if you don't feel anything or notice any difference with this exercise, don't despair. It takes a while to develop sensitivity to sound. Like all other intuitive skills it evolves through patience and practice.

Another tool that is useful in working with sound is a set of tuning forks. The vibrations from a tuning fork give a stronger, more focused energy than the more diffuse vibrations of the voice. They are well worth both the expense and the effort it takes in learning to use them. To activate a tuning fork, strike it against something hard, such as a scrap piece of wood, and hold it as close as possible to the stone or your body.

Our next step will be to establish resonance with tones and color using tuning forks or toning. To make the process easier you can program seven clear quartz crystals with the basic seven colors, using visualization or color filters.[2] Then try to match a tone for each color, holding the crystal as in the previous exercise, to establish a resonance for each color and tone. This is the system that works best for us:

red	C	blue	G
orange	D	indigo	A
yellow	E	violet	B
green	F		

Here is another system of resonances that comes from Alice Bailey's work with the seven rays. You might find this system more suited to your own beliefs:

red	C	blue	B
orange	G	indigo	A
yellow	E	purple-violet	F
green	D		

Next you can use the tuning forks for the minor notes of the scale, matching them with the color filters. Here are the resonances we use:

red	C	light sky blue	G
red-orange	C#	deep blue	G#
orange	D	indigo (blue-violet)	A
gold	D#	rose-purple	A#
yellow	E	violet	B
green	F	light rose-lavender	hi C
turquoise	F#		

We now introduce the idea of a "dominant frequency" or "soul tone." *Everything in nature, including gemstones and humans, has a dominant frequency, or soul tone, that expresses spiritual qualities related to its highest purpose.*

To find your particular soul tone, we have found it helpful to work in the range above hi C. Look for a tone which creates a "current" connecting you to the Earth and to your Higher Self. It will resonate all through you and feel both balancing and very expanding.

Each of your chakras also has a tone which relates to your individual lessons and purpose in this life. *This personal chakra tone will expand the chakra and connect it with your other chakras in a circuit.* We found that the personal tones work more quickly because they are more finely tuned to your energy system.

In becoming sensitive to sound it can be helpful to find your own personal chakra tones. Here is a way we used to find these tones:

1. Place a clear quartz crystal on your root chakra and tone or use the tuning fork for C.

2. Repeat the process using C# and try to determine which tone amplifies your energies and stimulates your chakras in a circuit. Continue through the rest of the chakras.

3. Here are some possibilities for you to try:

root	C, C#
lower abdomen	C#, D, D#
solar plexus	D#, E, F
heart	F, F#, G
throat	G, G#, A
third eye	A, A#, B
crown	A#, B, hi C

To find the dominant frequency or soul tone for a gemstone, try these steps:

1. Become relaxed and clear your mind of preconceptions. Become open and receptive and attune yourself to the stone.

2. Place the stone on a clear quartz crystal cluster for amplification. Use tuning forks to find the dominant frequency by holding the vibrating tuning fork to the stone and asking, "Is this my soul tone?" Be aware of how the tone resonates

in your body. You can also tone the sound through a crystal instead of the tuning forks.

3.   For verification and further discrimination, hold the stone in your hand and make tones until you find the one that resonates most deeply in your body. You can also hold the tuning fork to the stone in your hand.

We give our perceptions on soul tones in the discussions of the individual stones. We found that the soul tone of a gemstone does not always agree with its color. This is because the visible color we see represents only one aspect of its energy. Perhaps an analogous example is that your outer personality reflects only one aspect of your inner nature and purpose. The soul tone is more closely related to the particular spiritual qualities of the stone, as well as to the chakra or chakras for which it has an affinity. This concept will be discussed later on in this chapter.

A stone may resonate to more than one tone because each stone has a range of qualities in addition to its visible color. When you want the soul tone, you must focus your intuitive attention on receiving that information. Also, the composition of the stone affects the soul tone. For example, chryscolla is often found intergrown with quartz, malachite, and turquoise, so its soul tone can vary within the range of a whole tone.

Sound can be utilized to clear and charge your gemstones. Here are two approaches that we have used for clearing:

1.   Use your voice or a tuning fork and a crystal, and sound a tone that is a half-tone lower than the soul frequency. Visualize the stone being cleared. You may need to make the tone several times before the stone clears. For example, if the soul tone of the stone is an F, you might clear it with an E.

2.   When you have utilized the stone on a chakra, you can clear the stone by giving the personal chakra tone. Visualize the stone being cleared when you make the tones. For example, if you utilized the stone on your heart, and your personal heart tone is F#, then you would sound that tone. It is important to check the stone to see whether it needs another tone to be totally cleared.

To charge the stone, sound its soul tone, focusing your awareness on the stone being charged. With a tuning fork one sounding may be all that is needed. With your voice you may need more repetitions of the tone. If the soul tone of the stone is F, you would utilize that tone. With practice and patience you can learn to discriminate how the sounds affect your gemstones.

Your beliefs will affect your intuitive perceptions. Therefore, it is useful to keep records of your discoveries in order to compile data to help you understand your perceptions. As our own discrimination has become more finely tuned, we have changed our perceptions of some of the third eye and crown stones. We expect to do so again, because we know that this is an evolving process.

The rutilated quartz Deva closes with this explanation of the healing process with sound:

> "Each part of your being creates its own sound that indicates a normal flow of life-force energies. When I sense discordant vibrations coming from an area, I lock into the frequency that takes me directly to the areas needing my essence. I then help to restore the normal sound. You have the capacity to be a most infinitely beautiful symphony."

PERSPECTIVE THREE—CHAKRA AND SUBTLE BODY AFFINITIES

We have described in Chapter 2 how the aura consists of layers or subtle bodies. In our system we refer to three subtle bodies. It is most comfortable to work with the etheric subtle body, which is about one-quarter inch to two or three inches above the physical body. Stones placed on the body directly affect the etheric level. We sense the emotional and mental subtle bodies to be from three to four inches to about a foot above the physical body. The spiritual subtle body (or bodies) extends from about a foot to two or three feet from the physical body.

Although a stone can affect all of the subtle bodies, each stone has a particular affinity with one or more subtle bodies and one or more chakras. These affinities are related to their spiritual purpose. When you hold a stone, it will work most strongly with the subtle body or bodies where it has an affinity, and you may feel its energy in different ways. As a hypothetical example, you might notice that physically, your circulation seems speeded up, and mentally and emotionally, you feel more determined to focus on your goals. You might notice a sensation of heat in your right shoulder and solar plexus, where you have carried some fear about moving ahead. The stone is infusing its energy throughout your subtle body system to restore balance.

When you place a stone on a chakra, you will affect the etheric body even more strongly. You will also affect the emotional, mental, and spiritual issues involved at that chakra. Placing stones on various chakras helps to direct life force energy for balancing in all of the subtle bodies, resulting in a more powerful physical realignment.

The relationship between the chakras and the stones can also help you understand the qualities of stones as they relate to personal issues. We followed the method given below to determine the chakra and subtle body affinities of a stone:

1. It is easiest to work with a partner, but you can also try this on your own.

2. In addition to the gemstone, you will need a large clear quartz crystal which you will hold in your sending hand, and a smaller clear quartz crystal which will be placed on the body. You will also need gem water or a gem essence for each stone, for optimal amplification of the qualities (See Chapter 5).

3. It helps to practice a meditation or breathing technique that aligns your chakras. This is because the chakras that need energy may respond to a stone whether or not they have an affinity with it. With practice you can learn to tell the difference between a chakra affinity and a chakra that is taking in life-force energy.

4. Put a drop of the gem water on the tip of both crystals.

5. Begin at the root chakra and place the small crystal so that it is pointing toward the stone. Hold the larger crystal in your sending hand with the point toward your fingertips. (If you are working with a partner, they will hold the large crystal in their sending hand.)

6. Rotate your hand-held crystal counterclockwise about one or two inches above the root chakra at the etheric level and sense the energy. Your receiving hand is held palm up.

7. Next, rotate the crystal about four or five inches above the root at the emotional and mental level.

8. Finally, rotate the crystal about a foot or more above the body at the spiritual subtle body level. Compare the energy sensations. At the root chakra you can tell which of the subtle bodies the stone will affect most strongly.

9. Place the stone on the lower abdomen chakra and repeat the three rotations. Continue the process until you have checked all the chakras. At one or more chakras you will notice more tingling and a stronger sense of the qualities, as though the chakra has come to life. You may also notice energy sensations at all three subtle body levels.

If you try this and sense very little, repeat the process after you have worked with the stones in your own way. It takes practice to increase your sensitivity.

Our perceptions of chakra and subtle body affinities are given with each stone in Part Two. At the end of this chapter you will find an illustration of chakra locations (figure 3–1), as well as a summary of the meanings for each chakra (figure 3–2). At the end of Chapters 8 and 9 you will find charts that list the chakra affinities and soul tones of the stones (figures 8–15, 8–16, 9–13, 9–14). You may find over a period of time that your perceptions about chakra affinities change as you continue to receive guidance from the gemstones. As you grow you will work with stones in different ways.

THE CHAKRAS

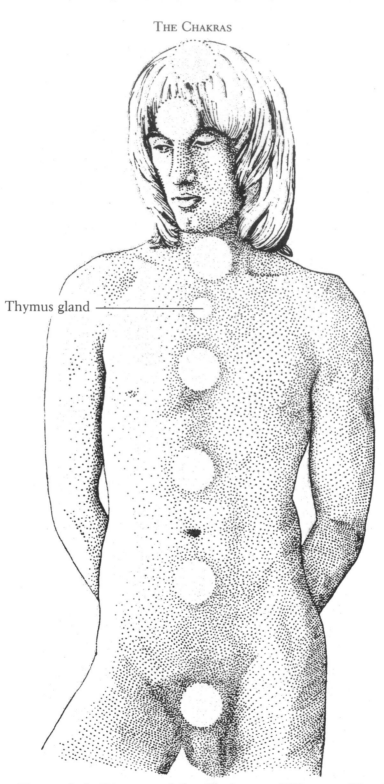

Thymus gland

FIGURE 3–1. Diagram of the Chakras and Thymus Gland

FIGURE 3–2. Summary of Chakra Information

CHAKRA	MEANING	LOCATION	AFFIRMATIONS
ROOT	Physical vitality: Basic will to be.	Base of the spine/ pubic bone	"I honor the natural physical vitality of my body and take care of it wisely." "I AM and the world welcomes me." "I live courageously, taking action to express my being."
LOWER ABDOMEN OR SPLEEN	Connecting with others through your feelings. Assimilating and letting go of your experience.	Midway be-tween navel and pubic bone	"I assimilate right understanding through my feelings and senses." "I welcome change and freely let go of what I don't need." "I am enough." "I trust the universe to supply my abundance and prosperity."
SOLAR PLEXUS	Developing self-confi-dence and building per-sonal power.	Two inches above the navel	"I own my strength and power." "I appreciate all the wonderful qualities that make me unique."
HEART	Developing compassion for all, especially yourself.	Heart	"I accept myself fully as I am." "I am truly loved."
THROAT	Speaking your truth creatively. Giving service.	Throat	"I now say what needs to be said." "I value and express my creativity." "My purpose is to serve others with my unique gifts."
THIRD EYE	Regulator and catalyst. Seat of your intuitive knowing.	Brow, midway between and slightly above the eyelashes	"I now release early and past-life experiences which do not serve my highest good." "I accept responsibility for creating my reality." "My intuitive connection with my Higher Spiritual Na-ture is expanding and becoming clear."
CROWN	Merging with your basic identity of God/ Goddess/All That Is.	Top of head	"I merge with the unity of all life." "I act in alignment with my Higher Spiritual Nature."

4 | Learning About Gem Energy: The Healing Process and the Four Elements

THIS CHAPTER EXPLAINS two final perspectives for viewing gemstone energy. Our fourth pespective involves perceiving the functional relationship between gemstones and thoughts and emotions. Jonathan and I believe that healing is a process which involves releasing imbalanced thoughts and feelings, incorporating new beliefs, and expanding into new levels of awareness.

Our fifth perspective involves relating the qualities of a stone to one of the Four Elements. This can allow you to develop a way to further describe *how the energy moves and its spiritual qualities.*

PERSPECTIVE FOUR—HEALING WITH THE THREE-STEP PROCESS

To be human is to experience your essential vulnerability. How do you keep from being swept under the tides of incomprehensible happenings and painful experiences? An age-old solution to this question is having compassion for yourself and others. The way of compassion takes lifetimes to learn. However, you can turn for help to the Kingdoms of Nature.

You can begin by recognizing that whether or not you acknowledge it, all of us carry pain. When something painful happens to you, you inevitably ask: "Why me?" When you are young you answer this question to the best of your understanding, but often you do not draw the correct conclusion. "Something is wrong with me," "I am basically unlovable," or "It was my fault," are erroneous conclusions that seem to make sense at the time. These false beliefs are empowered by the painful emotions of the experience. Until they are released and resolved, this emotional energy is locked into your physical and subtle bodies, restricting the flow of positive life-force energy on all levels: physical, emotional, mental, and spiritual. If the experience is an extremely painful memory, you may block the memory from your conscious mind, and attempt to resolve it by forgetting it. The memory then becomes stored in your subconscious mind, where you may carry it for the rest of your life and into future lifetimes, until it is resolved. This is partly the basis of karma; you create opportunities in this lifetime to resolve the false conclusions of the past.

One of my early past-life regressions helped me understand a prior relationship with a particular man. At the time we shared an interest in pioneer buildings and working with wood, and I depended on him for advice in practical matters. However, there were difficulties in our emotional relationship, and I often wondered why we were drawn together. We both knew that it was a temporary affair. In the regression I discovered that he had been my father in a previous lifetime when we had homesteaded in Tennessee. My mother (his wife) had died when I was two or three. I remember that I was angry with him for never sharing or talking about that grief, and I was estranged from him in that life. In the regression I forgave him and shared the mutual grief with him. Afterward it was though a cord had been cut. I had a sense of being totally at peace with this relationship and its purpose.

We often draw painful experiences into our present lives that are based on beliefs such as, "I'm always a victim." Sometimes these experiences are an attempt at resolution, and sometimes they are the perpetuation of a belief that has continued over lifetimes. The keys for resolution are also present in some manner, and you must choose to look for them.

The first step in our three-step model of healing is to clear negative emotions and beliefs. In order to do this you must first become aware of your beliefs. You must be brave enough to allow the painful feelings that empower your beliefs to surface. This can be a difficult process because you are very vulnerable when you express your deepest feelings and can be hurt by a lack of support or acceptance. Often, rather than risking being hurt again you choose to be silent and try to forget, much to the detriment of your physical and emotional health. It is helpful for you to understand your vulnerability so that you can create the necessary support.

A painful emotion, like "dis-ease" in the physical body, is a call for help and attention to an experience that needs resolution and compassion. *Expressing an emotion is actually a release of pain* or blocked energy that often illuminates a particular memory and the negative belief attached to it. For example, when I have examined the experience of feeling ignored by a former friend, I have discovered that beneath my anger at the friend is grief. That grief came from assuming that the cause of our separation was that there was something wrong with me. After expressing my feelings and releasing some of the blocked emotional energy, I could then see more clearly what I needed to affirm. The combination of new understanding and released tension healed the situation.

The idea that expressing emotions is a sign of weakness has significantly contributed to our lack of well-being. This idea is part of the male belief system in our culture and contributes to a great deal of unnecessary suffering. When we hold feelings inside and try to ignore them, we become more emotionally insensitive, unable to feel and express deep joy, and less able to understand the needs of others.

A key to clearing emotional pain and becoming more aware

of your limiting beliefs is compassion and self-acceptance. You often wish to tell your troubles to someone else, so that you can receive a bit of Unconditional Love and compassion. We need to encourage each other to listen to the unspoken words of doubt and discouragement, express our emotional pain, and give acceptance and love. You need to encourage yourself to merge with the compassion that is within you. Compassion can be visualized and felt as a friend, a Guardian Angel, a free-spirited child, a spiritual teacher such as Christ, or in any manner you wish. As you continue to ask for compassion and self-acceptance as part of the release process, the emotional pain lessens and experiences can be resolved.

The various Kingdoms of Nature, including the Mineral Kingdom, are another source of compassion and self-acceptance. Each stone is a unique expression of Unconditional Love, and you can experience that Love once you learn to merge with stones on a spiritual level. Depending on how you choose to work with their energies at a given time, stones can help you to release and heal emotional pain.

The process of clearing negative beliefs and emotions can be described in terms of energy flow. *Imbalance can be sensed as blocked energy; the clearing of this blocked energy is a phenomenon of dispersal which results in the restoration of flow.* It is possible to sense which stones are particularly helpful in the clearing and releasing process by noting whether their energy disperses or clears in some manner. These stones help clear a pathway for subsequent building and expansion by working with dense, blocked energy. Be aware of the manner in which the energy of a stone moves in your body and psyche, and see whether you are guided to "let go" in some manner. You can also use a pendulum and ask, "Are you useful in the clearing process of helping me become aware of and release imbalanced patterns?"

It is interesting to note that the function of many medicinal herbs which help you release toxins in different ways is essentially one of clearing. You need only make a conscious effort to ask for help from the Kingdoms of Nature and it is gladly given.

The next step in healing is an *infusing or building process.* This step, which is often integrated with clearing and release, involves building new and positive ways of thinking to replace the incorrect, imbalanced patterns. This can be liked to putting a new record on the record player. *It is necessary not only to express and release emotional energy, but to identify and change the negative beliefs.* Otherwise, it is possible to get stuck in the emotional pain. The building process takes effort and patience because it is easier to think and act in the old ways. Working with written and spoken affirmations is one of the best ways to build new confidence. Building is also an expansion process in which you go beyond your limitations and travel in new territory, doing things that you might not have dreamed possible earlier.

Once again, *compassion* and *self-acceptance* are key elements. Compassion for yourself and others gives you patience, because building is a step-by-step process. Sometimes, with our increased technology, we want immediate growth and admire people who can do things quickly. All the Kingdoms of Nature teach you that growth is gradual. You need to cultivate persistence and determination as well as delight in being in the moment. Once again, you must accept yourself as you are. The unique healing qualities of stones can be your spiritual building blocks, just as their physical forms give you additional vitality.

In terms of energy movement, building stones infuse and expand, rather than disperse. There can be a sense of heightened well-being on all levels, a stepping-up of physical energies, or an increased appreciation of your unique individuality. This movement is more like a coming together and elevating, rather than a dispersal of energy. Many stones assist in both clearing and building, depending on how you work with their energies. This is particularly true of the stones that have an affinity with the third eye. However, normally they either clear or build more strongly, particularly in combination with certain other stones. In this life you are learning to affirm and express your unique purpose and service. Just as each stone expresses its individual beauty, you can express your unique "colors" with patience and enjoyment.

The third step after clearing and building is *spiritual expansion.* We describe these steps sequentially in order to make them easier to understand, but in reality they are interwoven. In releasing imbalances and building new thought patterns, you emphasize your own individuality and service. *Spiritually expansive energy lifts you out of your mind, emotions, and physical body and into a Unity with All Life.* As you merge with the Infinite Consciousness you expand beyond rational knowledge. Every stone can teach you about spiritual expansion because they are innately connected with Unconditional Love and Light. However, certain stones, such as clear quartz crystal, are bridges in helping you understand that your own Goodness is part of the larger beauty of All That Is. The energy from these stones is very light, more finely tuned, and sometimes more difficult to describe. *It is a building energy that works at higher levels of spiritual awareness.*

We can illustrate the concept of the three-step healing process with a frequency band. This is like a color spectrum, with the densest energy on the left and the higher frequencies on the right. There are no sharp delineations in this band. Instead, the band illustrates a gradual flow of energies from left to right.

FIGURE 4–1. The Frequency Band

Clearing	Building and Infusing	Spiritual Expansion

Stones have specialties according to whether they help you disperse dense imbalanced energy, build balanced energy, or move into higher frequencies of energy. In Part Three, Chapter 6, we will expand the use of this frequency band.

Integrated with your growth process of clearing, building and spiritually expanding your understanding is the need for *grounding*. During times of change it can be helpful to focus on what supports and roots you. This may be a familiar routine or a special place to which you keep returning. That which grounds you is like a *core of balance* from which you release or expand.

Stones can serve as grounders or stabilizers because of their dense physical form and their function as a foundation for physical life. Certain stones play an important role in helping you integrate your awareness, honor your physical body, and focus on the daily tasks of living.

PERSPECTIVE FIVE—THE FOUR ELEMENTS OF NATURE

In working with stones, it can be helpful to relate their qualities to the energies of the Four Elements. To illustrate this I will give a practical example from my life. We were making regular visits to a small town park in which part of the walking path wound along a creek. I would listen to the sound of the water and imagine it flowing through me, carrying away with it various frustrations and thoughts that I wished to release. Having worked with water in this way I can now *feel* it flowing through me with all its cooling, fluid qualities. I am aware of what kinds of thoughts occur to me. Sometimes it is the idea that things are always changing. This thought sometimes occurs to me when I feel stuck. Sometimes I cry and feel the water as part of my tears, and I become particularly aware of this movement. The flowing water itself seems to be affirming my release and acknowledgment of pain. Sometimes the water seems very healing, as though it is a liquid lotion bathing me with loving hands. At other times I feel soothed and still. My relationship with water continues to change, and as I open to its qualities, I am able to receive what I need.

You can relate to any element of Nature's Kingdoms in this way. The perceptions you receive relate to your own beliefs, your own intuitive language, and what you need at any given time. The Elements heal on all levels because they are essential forms of life-force energy.

On the physical level you receive Earth energy from the foods you eat. This helps build the form of your physical body. For this reason it is important to eat natural, unprocessed foods so that you receive the maximum amount of life-force energy. Water is used externally for cleansing. Herbal baths and swimming revitalize the etheric energy field. Your body is over seventy percent water. Water taken internally, in the form of herbal teas, for example, also strengthens the energy fields.

Anyone who has practiced deep breathing as part of a transformational discipline knows the revitalizing effects of the air we breathe. *Prana* is a Sanskrit term for breath and "life-force energy." *Pranayama*, or regulated yogic breathing, is considered to be a gateway to expanded consciousness on all levels.

Sunlight (fire on the physical level) is a source of vitamin D essential to human health.

On the emotional and mental levels it is helpful to think of the Elements as *movements* of energy that instill qualities associated with their movement. As you visualize the Elements, notice how the energy moves in your body. Just as I worked with the creek water, you can work with the movement of any Element. The next time you are out on a windy day, find out from which direction the wind is blowing. Then experiment with different types of thoughts and find which feel most comfortable to you. For example, we found that winds that come from the North or West are particularly good for releasing thoughts and purifying your being. When you stand in winds from the South and East you can affirm new growth and expansion.

Several years ago as we walked on a nearby frozen lake, we discovered that ice is very helpful in clearing thoughts. As we stood, we focused on a difficult situation and concentrated on releasing our imbalanced thoughts until our minds were clear and the pain was gone. Ice seems to disperse energy quickly and intensely, possibly because of the density of the water. After we stepped off the ice and were back in the woods, we were aware of the contrast between the clearing intensity of the ice and the stability of the earth.

Snow also disperses energy, but in a gentler manner. Its physical whiteness and stillness seem to work well with thoughts of emptying the mind and purifying the energy system.

The Elements can teach you spiritually about your larger purpose in life. By merging with each Element, you can affirm being in harmony with Nature. By noticing which Element seems most meaningful to you, you can receive guidance about the direction to take in your growth.

From the Earth Element you learn to accept the sacred responsibility that you have as a steward for our precious Earth.

You learn how to properly and continuously align your energies with the Earth so that you can maintain a centeredness and balance as you follow your path. As with all the Elements you come to appreciate the beauty and perfection of the smallest forms of life you see on the Earth. *Earth qualities are deepening, centering, focusing, and stabilizing.*

By merging with the Water Element you can perceive ways to integrate your sensitivity through the use of the emotional body. You can let go of conditional responses to life experiences and move towards Unconditional Love and greater acceptance of self and others. You understand the aspect of feeling which exists beyond the physical level and allows a true expansion of your senses to occur. *Water qualities are flowing, surrendering, harmonizing, and accepting.*

By merging with Air you learn how to be spiritually mindful and how to utilize the energies of the mind for the highest good of all concerned. You move from a space of "me-ness" to one of encompassing the infinite totality of All That Is. *Air energies are emptying and uplifting.*

By merging with Fire you learn a purposeful focus of the life-force energy. On the Earth Plane it is sometimes referred to as power. What you learn is how to take a concept and give it greater clarity and discernment through proper utilization of your mind and will. *Fire qualities are purifying, stimulating, expansive, and action-oriented.*

The Elements of Earth, Water, Air, and Fire (sun) are necessary for your physical life on this Planet. You must learn that their spiritual qualities are necessary for your spiritual life as well.

PART TWO

The

Individual Gemstones

In Part One we acquainted ourselves with the Mineral Kingdom and reviewed five perspectives which can give insight into the spiritual qualities and purposes of the stones. Now that your perceptual tools have been sharpened, you are ready to know the individual stones. Meeting a stone is like making a friend. The true depth and beauty of a friend is revealed through the shared experience of struggles as well as the simple pleasures of life. These friends have much to give if you ask them to share with you.

When you meet a friend you may first notice their outer appearance, and ask where they live. So first we give you the *physical aspects* of the stone. Then we listen to the innermost essence of the stone in the *Devic channeling*. When you are attuning yourself to the spiritual qualities of a stone, you are attuning to the Deva of that stone. The Consciousness of every mineral is linked to an interconnected Higher Order of Beings, so that when you are connected with an individual Deva, you have access to many levels of wisdom and understanding. The Deva explains the spiritual qualities and purpose of the stone.

We then share with you our own perceptions of the perspectives given in Part One. The section on *spiritual aspects* contains the soul tone, the chakra and subtle body affinities, an energy focus for healing, and a descriptive Element. Note that in the chakra affinities (1) indicates a primary affinity and (2) indicates a secondary affinity. The different perspectives, as well as the Devic channeling, provide clues about ways to relate the stones to your everyday life, which we describe in the section on *co-creating with the gemstone*. Co-creating refers to wearing the stone, holding it, placing it on the body, meditating with it, or taking in its essence. A *gem essence* is an infusion of the gem's energies in pure water and alcohol, for the purpose of internal consumption. (In Part Three, Chapter 6, you will find a discussion of how to make and utilize gem essences.) Finally we end with an *affirmation* for each gemstone that captures the essence of its purpose.

Certain stones such as galena, pyrite, and rutilated quartz have a more generalized or broadly focused energy than other minerals. This broadly focused energy makes these stones more versatile in their use. In this respect they are like the metals copper, gold, and silver, which are described at the end of Part Two. The metals are also more broadly focused and versatile in their use, which makes them ideal partners with other stones in jewelry.

To get to know your stones, it helps to become familiar with them through your own intuitive process. Use this part of the book as another viewpoint or reference, rather than the definitive word on a particular stone. Let us now meet some new friends.

5 | Individual Gemstones and Metallic Elements

THE GEMSTONES

AMAZONITE

Physical Aspects

Amazonite, or amazon stone, as it is sometimes called, is an opaque, blue-green potassium feldspar. Its chemical composition is potassium aluminum silicate. It has a hardness of 6–6½ and a triclinic crystalline structure. In the U.S. there are deposits in Colorado, Pennsylvania, and Virginia. Amazonite is also found in Russia, Brazil, Malagasy Republic, and India. It is usually cut in cabochon or round for bead necklaces.

The Amazonite Deva

''I provide a sense of continuity and understanding between the world of the body and the world of the spirit. Through my energies you may experience hope, joy, and transcendence. I can help you give meaning and value to your life regardless of what you have chosen to do, so that your transitions are more peaceful.

''Did you know that all lifestreams enter the Earth plane with the highest ideals of what they seek to do? I speak to those of you who have come a long way in space and time to be here on the Earth plane, and to those of you who contemplate a premature exit from the physical vehicle. Sometimes you may feel a sense of disillusionment, and perhaps even seek to leave the Earth plane, because you feel you have accomplished nothing. I help you to bless what you have done, rather than mourn what the goal was to have been.

''To all of you I say that through spiritual expansion, you will come to know and understand the limitlessness of your being and how truly multifaceted you are. Your relationship to life itself undergoes a transformation and you see that you are part of Infinity, connected with All That Is. Your sense of spiritual compassion and understanding increases as you witness numerous paths that lead to total Unity with All. Your task is to make this Earth a heaven, and to heal that which is of Earth, so that what you seek will already be with you.''

Spiritual Aspects

Soul Tone: A, A#. Most of our stones test A.
Chakra Affinities: Third Eye (1), Thymus Gland (1), Crown (2)*
Subtle Body Affinities: Spiritual (Affects all subtle bodies on the Thymus Gland)
Energy Focus: Spiritual Expansion
Element: Air

Co-creating with Amazonite

Amazonite can be held in meditation to lift you beyond your personal self and help you merge with spirit. If you fear out-of-body experiences, amazonite can calm this fear. If you know of someone who is terminally ill, that person can benefit from having the energies of amazonite in his or her presence.

*Note: (1) indicates primary affinity, (2) indicates secondary affinity.

Affirmation

"I am protected by the Light as I move through transitions in my life, and I bless what I have accomplished."

AMBER

Physical Aspects

Amber is organic in origin, consisting of the fossilized resin of the pine tree, *Pinus succinifera*. It was formed during the Eocene period fifty to seventy million years ago. It has a hardness of 2½ and an amorphous crystalline structure. In color, amber most commonly ranges from light yellow and gold to brown and red. It often has inclusions of insects and parts of plants. There are large reserves of amber along the shores of the Baltic Sea, where it can be picked up on the beaches and in shallow water after heavy storms. There is also a well-known deposit in Poland, some minor deposits along the Atlantic coast in the U.S., and in the Dominican Republic.

The Amber Deva

''I teach you that physical vitality is maintained through a lightness of spirit. Sometimes you seek instantaneous results and then you become weighed down with a sense that the growth process will take forever. I help you elevate your thoughts to a different level, where you can see the meaning in what is taking place without judging the time and effort involved. Although it is not my only function, I encourage laughter. Laughter frees heavy energy so that you breathe more freely and lightly. You are continually evolving at different stages in your soul's development. Some aspects are accelerating more rapidly than other aspects. Be patient with who you are right now and accept yourself without judgment. Doing this will give you a sunny, light disposition that can see the humor in things.''

Spiritual Aspects

Soul Tone: C̆

Chakra Affinities: Root (1), Lower Abdomen (1), Solar Plexus (1)

Subtle Body Affinities: Etheric, Emotional/Mental, Spiritual

Energy Focus: Building

Element: Air

Co-creating with Amber

When you feel that life is a burden or a struggle, or you feel weighted down with responsibility, amber with its uplifting energies teaches you to walk lightly. It can help you see life with more humor and to find the joy in each step of the way. Amber can create a happy balance between the affairs of daily living and the movement toward higher mental and spiritual expansion.

Affirmation

"I build my physical vitality through lightness of spirit."

AMETHYST

Physical Aspects

Amethyst is a member of the quartz family, a silicon dioxide with a hardness of 7 and a trigonal crystalline structure. In its crystalline form amethyst ranges from pale to deep violet. Its color is thought to be due to minute traces of iron. Amethyst quartz is a rougher, more compact form of amethyst that is striped with milky quartz and often polished. Some amethysts can lose their color in daylight but the original color can be restored by X-ray radiation. Amethysts are often found in geodes in alluvial deposits. A geode is a nodule of siliceous volcanic rock containing quartz crystals or quartz agate inside. The most important deposits of amethyst are in Brazil, Uruguay, and the Malagasy Republic.

The Amethyst Deva

''My purpose is to heighten your spiritual awareness and to help you remember the Divinity that is you.

Self is viewed from a higher spiritual perspective. Letting go of your old ways of thinking about self and others, and becoming One with your Divine Essence, transforms the you that was into the you that is. The process of transition, whether in the physical body at death, or in your mind during the growth process, is merely a change in your level of awareness that can bring you greater self-fulfillment. My transformation of your energies is truly a purification and a cleansing, and with my peace, you need not fear death in any form."

Spiritual Aspects

Soul Tone: B
Chakra Affinities: Crown (1), Thymus Gland (1), Third Eye (2)
Subtle Body Affinities: Spiritual, Etheric, Emotional/Mental
Energy Focus: Clearing
Element: Air

Co-creating with Amethyst

With its purifying energies, amethyst helps clear and transform energies in the environment where it is placed. Therefore it is an aid to help you release imbalanced energies during the day, or protect yourself in an imbalanced environment. Amethyst has a calming effect that helps you release unnecessary thoughts. The sense is one of being purified and freed of burdens. Holding an amethyst or taking its essence can be a way of preparing yourself for spiritual work. Amethyst can also be used to help you understand your dreams. Because it works mainly with the spiritual body, it can be helpful in utilizing other stones or practices in conjunction with amethyst specifically to affect your conscious mind, emotions, or physical body. What it does is to provide a "light space" where you can get your bearings. Amethyst can help you remember that you are more than the principal actor or actress in your life drama. You are indeed the Light.

Affirmation:

"I release all need for self-identity."

AQUAMARINE

Physical Aspects

Aquamarine, like emerald, is a member of the beryl family. It is named for the resemblance of its color to sea water. Aquamarine is an aluminum beryllium silicate that gets its color from traces of iron. It has a hardness of 7½–8 and a trigonal crystalline structure. Rough aquamarine crystals are fairly common and they have a striated appearance, somewhat like tourmaline. Lighter aquamarine is sometimes heated to change it to a darker blue. Aquamarine is found in the pegmatites and coarse granites of Brazil, Malagasy Republic, and the U.S., as well as numerous other locations.

The Aquamarine Deva

''I encourage you to perceive your daily service as a way to care for others and grow spiritually. When you feel in conflict about whether what you are doing has meaning, I can help you understand how you are fulfilling the spiritual purpose in your life. My energies give a sense of continuity that can reassure you when you are discouraged about whether or not you are accomplishing what you have set out to do. I tell you to trust that what you share with others in your daily service has value and meaning, especially when you see your work as a way of giving Unconditional Love to others.''

Spiritual Aspects

Soul Tone: G, F#. Darker aquamarines test F#. Pale light aquamarines test G.
Chakra Affinities: Throat (1), Heart (2)
Subtle Body Affinities: Emotional/Mental, Spiritual, Etheric
Energy Focus: Building
Element: Water

Co-creating with Aquamarine

When you are feeling discouraged or your work feels empty, aquamarine can help you find deeper satisfaction and healing in your daily work. Aquamarine teaches you to value yourself and what you give to others. It expands a limited view of the results of your efforts. The essence is both reassuring and uplifting, because it helps you find spiritual fulfillment in everything you do.

Affirmation:

"I am reassured and uplifted by the knowledge that my work is my love made visible." (Inspired by Kahlil Gibran)

AVENTURINE

Physical Aspects

Aventurine is a green microcrystalline quartz with white and sparkly inclusions of hematite or mica which give a spangled appearance. Like other members of the quartz family, it is silicon dioxide, with a hardness of 7 and a trigonal crystalline structure. It is most often found in India, Brazil, and Russia.

The Aventurine Deva

"My energies encourage you to move from a limited vision of your capabilities to a more diverse exploration of your creative gifts. From the moment you decide to incarnate in a physical vehicle on Planet Earth, the process of exploring your personal reality begins. Do you seek experiences that are going to support a narrowly focused state of being or do you desire to embrace the broader facets of life? Sometimes you may be unaware of gifts and interests that you possess, and sometimes you stubbornly refuse to explore those gifts of which you are already aware. In order to truly understand and fulfill your spiritual purpose you must explore the possibilities. I can calm the apprehension and uncertainty that is behind a limited focus of what you can express. I build your self-worth by encouraging you to experience alternative ways of being in your world."

Spiritual Aspects

Soul Tone: E

Chakra Affinities: Solar Plexus (1), Lower Abdomen (1), Heart (2)

Subtle Body Affinities: Emotional/Mental, Spiritual, Etheric

Energy Focus: Building

Element: Water

Co-creating with Aventurine

Aventurine has a gentle, flowing expansiveness that helps you see that you can do more things than you thought you could do. It encourages exploration and creating in new ways. Aventurine could be helpful in career assessment and during transitions from functioning in one role to being called upon to act in new ways.

Affirmation:

"I expand my vision of who I can be."

AZURITE

Physical Aspects

Azurite is a basic copper carbonate with five percent water and a hardness of 3½–4. It belongs to the monoclinic system. As a secondary copper mineral it is often found with malachite and mined in copper deposits. It takes the form of a dense aggregate, small crystals, or spherical aggregate balls. The most well-known deposits are in the Urals in Russia, Australia, and in this country, in Arizona and Pennsylvania.

The Azurite Deva

''As I prepare the way for the Light through denser energy, my energies are those of change and purification. I help you to know and reprogram your subconscious mind so that your intuitive sensitivity is increased. I help you prepare for change through gradual adjustment so that there is a sense of safety and reassurance. In this way I also help you build your spiritual awareness beyond your five senses.

"There is another related purpose that I serve. When a soul has been out of a physical vehicle for some time and has decided to re-enter the Earth Plane, my energies are infused into the subconscious memory of the being to help alleviate the stress of moving into a denser environment.

"I can help you adjust your energies in a balanced manner from denser to finer levels of reality. I give both reassurance and a calm readiness."

Spiritual Aspects

Soul Tone: G#, Stones containing other minerals besides azurite may test G.
Chakra Affinities: Third Eye (1)
Subtle Body Affinities: Emotional/Mental, Spiritual, Etheric
Energy Focus: Clearing
Element: Water/Earth

Co-creating with Azurite

With its steady, deep, inward focus azurite is helpful for past-life work or for reprogramming your subconscious. It is a good stone for meditation because it will help clear and balance your third eye so that it can receive finer energies.

Affirmation

"I find peace as I release emotional ties from the past."

BLOODSTONE

Physical Aspects

Bloodstone, or heliotrope, as it is sometimes called, is an opaque, dark green chalcedony quartz with red spots of jasper. As a member of the quartz family it is silicon dioxide, with a trigonal crystal system and a hardness of 7. The most important deposits are in India, Australia, Brazil, China, and the U.S.

The Bloodstone Deva

"When your will is aligned with your spiritual purpose, I can affirm your perseverance in riding the waves that surface along the path. My energies can assist you in realigning with your spiritual purpose through clearing self-doubts caused by recent memories from present or past lives. Sometimes when there are things in your life that are inconsistent with where you want to be, you simply need to go further in the process toward continuity and balance. Inner power is built through steadily overcoming doubt and fear, and reaffirming what you came to do and learn in this life."

Spiritual Aspects

Soul Tone: C# or C. A bloodstone with more red will resonate to C. Stones that are mostly green resonate at C#.
Chakra Affinities: Root (1), Lower Abdomen (1), Solar Plexus (2)
Subtle Body Affinities: Emotional/Mental, Etheric, Spiritual
Energy Focus: Clearing
Element: Earth/Fire

Co-creating with Bloodstone

Bloodstone can give powerful strength and stamina during a seemingly endless period of difficulty, when there has been despair or loss of hope. Bloodstone helps you see a situation as a challenge and can aid you in clearing feelings of weakness or discouragement.

You can utilize the stone to clear self-doubts that are a result of present or past-life experiences. First, place bloodstone on the area of the body where blockage es experienced. Second, place a clear quartz crystal with bloodstone essence on the third eye, to facilitate memory, understanding, and release of the experience.

Bloodstone also has the capacity to clear scattered thoughts as you prepare to meditate.

Affirmation

"I affirm the power of my perseverance to see me through all situations."

BLUE LACE AGATE

Physical Aspects

Blue lace agate is a light blue, banded microcrystalline quartz, with a hardness of 7. Like other members of the quartz family it is composed of silicon dioxide and belongs to the trigonal crystal system. The most well-known agate deposits are in southern Brazil and northern Uruguay.

The Blue Lace Agate Deva

"Love needs to be the foundation of expression not only to your fellow humans, but to yourself as well. I urge you to speak honestly to yourself, yet without judgment. Whenever you speak in a positive, non-judgmental manner to yourself, this process opens the channel of sharing that can occur between you and other lifestreams. For example, having the spiritual gift of sensitivity means that you may experience things more deeply than other beings. How do you express this spiritual gift? Do you speak of the hardships that it occasionally brings with it into your life? Or do you speak of the opportunities that open, in order to be a healing catalyst for other lifestreams? Every action that you take in life is a reflection of your growth on your spiritual path. Be sure that what you speak is for your highest purpose and the highest purpose of the other. When this is done, you can be sure that what you say will reach that being where it is most needed at the present moment."

Spiritual Aspects

Soul Tone: G#
Chakra Affinities: Throat (1)

Subtle Body Affinities: Mental, Spiritual
Energy Focus: Building
Element: Earth

Co-creating with Blue Lace Agate

Blue lace agate strengthens a sense of calm centeredness that can help in social situations if you are inclined to draw attention to yourself through your speech. It encourages focus, discernment, and tact in speech, and discourages nervous habits of impulsive chatter or wandering speech. Blue lace agate would be a useful essence for building confidence in public speaking or in general social situations.

Affirmation

"I reflect calm inner certainty, as I speak with non-judgment and discernment."

CALCITE

Physical Aspects

Calcite is a calcium carbonate that comes in a variety of colors including red, green-blue, brown, and black. The clear variety is called Icelandic Spar. Calcite is soft as minerals go, with a Mohs' hardness of 3, so it is not generally used in jewelry. Like quartz, it belongs to the trigonal system, and because of its perfect rhombohedral cleavage, it is often sold in the rhombohedral shape. Calcite is the most common of all calcium carbonate minerals and is found in a variety of environments. Calcite is the main constituent of stalagmites and stalactites in limestone caverns. These are formed when water containing carbon dioxide in solution filters through limestone joints, where it evaporates and crystallizes in the shape of columns. Marble is a crystalline limestone consisting of calcite and dolomite in massive form.

We will discuss green, blue, and honey calcite.

The Green Calcite Deva

''I work in a cool, gentle, calming manner to ease the reverberations of shock or an overly volatile approach in some aspect of your life. I give you a peaceful sense of being in control of your experiences as well as a sense of safety and reassurance. I can help you bring your feelings into a more relaxed and central place so that you can clear what you need to with a minimum of discomfort. You may feel a lifting of burdens each time you work with my energies. Those of you who are highly sensitive and vulnerable can benefit from working with my energies.''

Green Calcite—Spiritual Aspects

Soul Tone: D
Chakra Affinities: Lower Abdomen (1), Heart (2)
Subtle Body Affinities: Emotional/Mental, Etheric
Energy Focus: Clearing
Element: Water

Co-creating with Green Calcite

Calcite is one of the clearing stones that balances and calms rather than stimulating or encouraging release. Green calcite essence is wonderful as a physical relaxant, especially if you have a churning stomach. If you are nervous and keyed up with minor emotional upsets, calcite will help you relax and calm down, with its soothing gentle energy. It is easy to imagine drifting in the water with calcite, because it also has a flowing quality.

Green Calcite Affirmation

"I release nervous tension and feel calm and relaxed."

Blue Calcite Deva

''Energy levels are being intensified within all life forms, and within Planet Earth herself. Many in the Human Kingdom, particularly those whose emotional, mental, and spiritual bodies are highly sensitive, may experience these active energies in a deep manner. When this occurs you may need to have a way to diffuse this impact on your energy system. That is my function. I help to calm your emotional and mental levels so that you can see clearly what action you may need to take in the experience. Where I sense that you are receiving some special benefit through the intensity of your experiences, my energies may just 'take the edge off the intensity,' so that its volatile nature is only minutely changed. Know that no lifestream within the Human Kingdom is ever able to experience more intensity of change than the energy system is capable of processing.''

Blue Calcite—Spiritual Aspects

Soul Tone: E
Chakra Affinities: Solar Plexus (1)
Subtle Body Affinities: Emotional/Mental, Etheric
Energy Focus: Clearing
Element: Water

Co-creating with Blue Calcite

You can take blue calcite when you feel overwhelmed with the intensity of change in your life. Blue calcite lessens the sense of trauma and helps you move through the changes with more peace.

Blue Calcite Affirmation

"I affirm safety and peace during times of intensity."

Honey Calcite Deva

''Whenever you are in an intense period of change and you wonder how you are going to make it through, my energies can give you that 'extra lift' to help you rise to the occasion.''

Honey Calcite—Spiritual Aspects

Soul Tone: D#
Chakra Affinities: Solar Plexus (1)
Subtle Body Affinities: Emotional/Mental, Etheric
Energy Focus: Clearing, Building
Element: Water

Co-creating with Honey Calcite

Honey calcite is helpful during intense periods of change in creating an optimistic strength. It is an aid when you feel disillusioned, tired, or burdened.

Honey Calcite Affirmation

"I remain optimistic during times of intensity."

CARNELIAN

Physical Aspects

Carnelian, sometimes spelled cornelian, is a member of the microcrystalline quartz family. Therefore it is silicon dioxide, with a hardness of 7 and a trigonal crystalline structure. Carnelian ranges from orange-red to orange-brown and various shades of gold. Many carnelians are agates from Brazil and Uruguay. Sometimes they are colored with ferrous nitrate solution to brighten them and show stripes. Natural carnelian has a cloudy distribution of color. Carnelian also comes from India, where the reddish hues are enhanced by exposure to the sun. We will talk about orange and yellow carnelian.

Orange Carnelian Deva

''The quality I share with the Human Kingdom is optimism. Being optimistic about your present learning space allows you to act more spontaneously and less fearfully in the tasks of your daily life. I do not enter your energy field with fiery enthusiasm. Rather, I encourage moderation and tolerance. Find the positive opportunities in each day and appreciate the small gifts that you give to others and to yourself. In this way we can work together in building your self-worth. Know always that all is well.''

Orange Carnelian—Spiritual Aspects

Soul Tone: D
Chakra Affinities: Lower Abdomen (1), Solar Plexus (1)
Subtle Body Affinities: Emotional/Mental, Etheric
Energy Focus: Building
Element: Earth

Co-creating with Orange Carnelian

With its cheerful vitality, orange carnelian can help you look on the brighter side of things when you are feeling gloomy or a little despondent. Orange carnelian's optimism can also help with decision-making, if you tend to feel irritated with the idiosyncrasies of others or the little mishaps in life. It stimulates you physically to act in moderation. You can also work with it for past-life exploration when intuitively guided to do so.

Orange Carnelian Affirmation

"I find something positive to enjoy in every aspect of my life."

Yellow Carnelian Deva

''Through my energies, your sensitivity to your environment is expanded. I help you to focus your energies into experiences that can have positive effects on your life. Life can truly take on new meaning as you open to the vibrant light quality that can be found within all things.''

Yellow Carnelian—Spiritual Aspects

Soul Tone: D#
Chakra Affinities: Solar Plexus (1), Lower Abdomen (2)

Subtle Body Affinities: Emotional/Mental, Etheric
Energy Focus: Building
Element: Earth

Co-creating with Yellow Carnelian

Yellow carnelian has a gentler, more refined vibration than orange carnelian. It continues the process begun by orange carnelian of viewing life more optimistically. Therefore, you might work with its essence after you have worked with orange carnelian. Yellow carnelian reassures you that all is flowing well, so that you can enjoy the process.

Affirmation

"I enjoy the gifts in my everyday life with all my senses."

CELESTITE

Physical Aspects

Celestite, or celestine, as it is sometimes called, is a transparent, bluish-white stone with a hardness of 3–3½. It is a strontium sulphate with an orthorhombic crystalline structure. Celestite is found in sedimentary rock deposits, principally in the U.S. Celestite was discovered in the excavating of the Erie Canal in New York, and it has also been found in Ohio, California, and Mexico.

The Celestite Deva

''The 'sacred space' is that inner place at the very core essence of your being where information is translated into 'knowing' prior to its expression. To function as a place where 'knowing' in its purest form can exist, the vibratory rate there must be at a level where pure light can be present at all times. My energy essence contains the tonal pattern of this sacred space and helps to clear it by infusing a greater light into it. Whatever happens in the sacred space determines the degree of openness that is present in the throat and third eye chakras. This in turn affects the state of balance on the physical level in those areas of your being. My work with the Human Kingdom in this capacity is ongoing in its nature, since the process of creation and change is essential to spiritual growth."

Spiritual Aspects

Soul Tone: G
Chakra Affinities: Throat (1), Third Eye (1)
Subtle Body Affinities: Mental, Spiritual, Etheric
Energy Focus: Clearing
Element: Air

Co-creating with Celestite

Celestite clears "left-brain chatter" so that you can connect with your Higher Guidance. It aids you in dispersing the memory of an incident that keeps playing like a broken record. Its calming effect relaxes and empties your mind for rest, meditation, or when you need a break from mental concentration. On an ongoing basis celestite can ease doubts coming from the rational mind when you are evaluating your paranormal experiences. With celestite you can better discern whether your guidance is coming from your desires or your Higher Wisdom.

Affirmation

"My mind is relaxed and open to connect with my Higher Guidance."

CHALCEDONY

Physical Aspects

Chalcedony is a name for the microcrystalline quartz group and is also used to describe a waxy, translucent stone that can be bluish-gray or white. In our work we use a white variety, which we will refer to as chalcedony. As a member of the quartz family, it is silicon dioxide with a trigonal structure and a hardness of 7. Because it is porous it can be dyed, so you may need to check and make sure that you have a natural piece. Chalcedony is widely distributed and is most commonly found in Brazil, India, Uruguay, and the Malagasy Republic.

The Chalcedony Deva

"I encourage you to express your emotional needs. When you do that, I can bring you calm and peace. If there has been one element lacking pure expression within the Human Kingdom, it is the expression of feelings. Ongoing spiritual expansion requires emotional openness. This does not mean that you internalize all forms of emotional energies that you are exposed to in your life experience. Instead, you learn to accept what is going to be a catalyst for your spiritual growth."

Spiritual Aspects

Soul Tone: Ranges from D to E, depending on how white it is, E being the tone for the whitest stones.
Chakra Affinities: Solar Plexus (1), Lower Abdomen (1)
Subtle Body Affinities: Emotional/Mental, Etheric
Energy Focus: Clearing
Element: Earth/Water

Co-creating with Chalcedony

Chalcedony asks you to be accountable to your own feelings and to be emotionally honest. Sometimes you may find yourself covering your feelings with a veneer that you have it all together, while simultaneously experiencing a sense of numbness or emotional tension. Chalcedony encourages you to express your feelings and to ask for the support you need. Its gentle, stimulating energy can help you move through times of sadness and regret.

Affirmation

"I trust the messages my feelings are giving me and I speak up for what I need."

CHRYSOCOLLA

Physical Aspects

Chrysocolla is an opaque, blue-green hydrous copper silicate with a hardness of 2–4. It belongs to the monoclinic crystal system and is often found with azurite and malachite as a by-product of copper mining. It has the property of sticking to the tongue, which can be a test of identification. Major deposits are in the southwestern United States, Chile, the Ural mountains in Russia, and Zaire. Chrysocolla often contains varying amounts of malachite and quartz, so it is an aggregate stone. Gem quality chrysocolla is called gem silica and is fairly expensive because it is rare. We have worked with both rough and polished chrysocolla.

The Chrysocolla Deva

''I teach you to follow the response that can be felt deeply within the heart, to ensure that you are truly aligned with your spiritual purpose. The greater the resistance that occurs in your heart when you are making choices in life, the more certainty there is that your actions are outside the dimensions of your spiritual purpose. When you find yourself hesitating or feeling uncertain about a particular direction, examine your intentions. Is it truly for the highest good of all concerned to move forward in the particular manner that you are proposing? When there is a sense of flow, continuity, and peace within your being, then you are truly aligned with the energies of your spiritual purpose. I tell you that your heart can be your closest companion and advisor as you choose your life path on the Earth Plane.''

Spiritual Aspects

Soul Tone: G, F#, or F depending on the amount of malachite or quartz in the individual stone. The greener stones vibrate to F, and the bluer stones resonate to F# or G.

Chakra Affinities: Throat (1), Heart (2)
Subtle Body Affinities: Emotional/Mental, Spiritual
Energy Focus: Clearing
Element: Water

Co-creating with Chrysocolla

Chrysocolla provides a reassuring encouragement that helps you move through fear in expressing your spiritual purpose. You can work with it during the process of finding more satisfying work, or beginning a new creative expression. Chrysocolla helps clear links with the past as you move into new areas of service, both in your outer and inner worlds. You may also become more aware of different ways to express yourself creatively in a practical manner.

Affirmation

"I listen to my heart, to find and affirm my spiritual purpose."

CHRYSOPRASE

Physical Aspects

Chrysoprase is an opaque, apple-green member of the microcrystalline quartz family. Its color comes from the trace mineral nickel, which is present with the basic silicon dioxide. Like other quartz, chrysoprase has a hardness of 7 and a trigonal crystalline structure. Gem quality chrysoprase comes from Australia, California, Oregon, and Brazil. It is sometimes colored artificially.

The Chrysoprase Deva

''Commit your energies to completing one process each day. Your small successes and accomplishments are just as significant as your major ones. Look for interrelationships between those things you have done and those in the planning stages. My energies encourage this practice, particularly when you have just completed something and aren't sure what to do next. Keep your conscious mind open to opportunities that may 'appear out of the blue.' Know that there is always a continuity of flow present between the completion of one stage of growth and the start of a new stage. Be patient with your flow and at peace with your process.''

Spiritual Aspects

Soul Tone: D
Chakra Affinities: Solar Plexus (1), Lower Abdomen (1)
Subtle Body Affinities: Emotional/Mental, Etheric, Spiritual
Energy Focus: Building
Element: Earth

Co-creating with Chrysoprase

Chrysoprase can aid you in relieving anxiety and apprehension as you move into the unknown. Its grounding stability gives a sense of continuity that helps you focus on the present moment.

Affirmation

"Completing one step at a time connects me with my inner roots and gives me a sense of continuity in my life."

CITRINE

Physical Aspects

Citrine is a yellow quartz. It is a silicon dioxide with a hardness of 7 and a trigonal crystalline structure. Many citrines are heat-treated amethysts or smoky quartzes. Brazilian amethyst turns a lemon-yellow at about nine hundred degrees fahrenheit, and dark yellow at about one thousand degrees fahrenheit. The heat-treated stones have a red tint to them. Natural citrine is a pale yellow and is less common. Large deposits of citrine are mined in Brazil and Madagascar.

The Citrine Deva

"Synthesis is a quality that I share with the Human Kingdom. I help you incorporate the input from your logical mind and your intuitive mind into your conscious belief system, so that you feel a sense of clarity and resolve. When you are working with your logical mind, I help you separate what is relevant from what is irrelevant, so that you have the key elements in focus. Unfortunately, your society teaches you to ignore your intuitive mind. By doing so you can throw yourself off balance. I strengthen your intuitive perceptions and help you utilize your information in a way that synthesizes the input from your different sources. When you use both your conscious and intuitive mind you are less likely to stew over a situation, and you will be calmer physically. Ultimately you will develop a greater peace of mind.

"I have one other comment that I wish to make. The Human Kingdom has taken it upon itself to alter the color emanations of the different minerals. Though I cannot change the procedure, I state most directly that I am opposed to all attempts to alter the molecular structure of any minerals. This viewpoint is shared by the other Devas wherever this misapplication of energies is occurring."

Spiritual Aspects

Soul Tone: E
Chakra Affinities: Solar Plexus (1), Third Eye (1)
Subtle Body Affinities: Mental, Spiritual, Etheric
Energy Focus: Building
Element: Air

Co-creating with Citrine

When you are feeling pulled by differing points of view, citrine can help you synthesize your understanding. Citrine can open the way for a unifying perspective that often comes from the intuitive mind. Citrine is helpful on an ongoing basis for mental clarity in communicating ideas to others, writing, and problem solving.

Affirmation

"I think and communicate clearly, synthesizing information from all levels of my being."

CORAL

Physical Aspects

Coral is one of the organic gem materials, consisting of the calcified skeletons of coral polyps. These polyps are tiny, primitive organisms that eventually attach themselves to previous coral growth and secrete a substance that is similar to calcite. The chemical composition of coral is calcium carbonate with magnesium carbonate and traces of organic substances. Coral has a hardness of 3–4 and a vitreous luster when polished. In the gem trade red, pink and, white corals are the most favored colors. Coral is sensitive to heat, acids, and hot solutions, and the color can fade when worn. Coral is worked with a saw, knife, and file rather than the standard polishing wheels. There are many imitations made from glass, plastic, and other minerals.

Coral is harvested by dragging nets across the sea beds. Unfortunately, this method destroys much valuable material. Coral is dredged in the Mediterranean and off the coasts of Italy, Algeria, Sicily, Spain, and Japan. We will discuss the white and red corals.

The White Coral Deva

"Infinite paths are available for those in the Human Kingdom to follow in the growth cycle each has chosen. It is only natural to want to make things better for those you feel close to. I am here to help you learn to value the unique being that you are. You no longer need to take it personally when people do not listen to what you are saying. With my energies to balance you, you can ask your Higher Self or the Higher Self of another, whether it is in his/her highest good for you to offer suggestions. I broaden your spiritual understanding by teaching you to forgive yourself and others when something has been shared that has not been for the highest good. Forgiveness is truly the quickest way to heal hurt and misunderstanding.

"My energies also strengthen you when you feel you are being told what to do by another. With me you can assimilate those energies that are helpful to you in your growth and release other energies without hurt or judgment. By not judging the gift that a person gives, you help to maintain the purity of its form. By not judging yourself you maintain your own purity and balance."

White Coral—Spiritual Aspects

Soul Tone: G, G# Both tones seem equally common.
Chakra Affinities: Throat (1)
Subtle Body Affinities: Emotional/Mental, Etheric, Spiritual
Energy Focus: Clearing
Element: Fire/Water

Co-creating with White Coral

When you are with family and friends, white coral can strengthen your self-esteem and help you clear judgment, frustration, and resentment relating to being told what to do. It can also aid you in letting go of the desire for recognition that can spur you on to give unwanted advice to others. White coral encourages you to affirm that you have something worthwhile to say, and to recognize yourself within.

White Coral Affirmation

"I listen to that which is for my highest good and I release all else."

The Red Coral Deva

"Each lifestream needs to adopt an independent nature when other beings question or are directly critical of choices that are made. You need to be free of judgment so that you can function in a purity of flow. My energies help you to remain connected to your path in this life, regardless of the external experiences that my present themselves in opposition to your actions. I help you to move forward decisively, once you have assimilated what you need for taking your next step.''

Red Coral—Spiritual Aspects

Soul Tone: E
Chakra Affinities: Solar Plexus (1)
Subtle Body Affinities: Emotional/Mental, Etheric, Spiritual
Energy Focus: Clearing
Element: Fire/Water

Co-creating with Red Coral

Red coral helps you resolve an experience where there has been conflict and criticism, and move forward decisively. It can clear the paralysis that can set in when you fear to make a move because of someone's disapproval. Sometimes the action you may need to take is to distance yourself from the source of confusion, and red coral can encourage you in this direction.

Red Coral Affirmation

"I honor both my own unique path and the unique paths of others, by taking decisive action without judgment."

DIAMOND

Physical Aspects

Diamond is pure carbon, with an isometric crystalline structure. Standing at 10 on the Mohs' scale, it is the hardest substance known. Only diamond will cut diamond. Diamond has a high ability to bend light (refraction) and to disperse light into its component colors. These properties are best brought out when the stone is cut and faceted. The brilliant cut, which has thirty-two facets plus the table (top flat surface) on the upper part, and twenty-four facets on the lower part, was especially developed to bring out the intense brilliance and fire of the diamond.

Diamonds form in igneous pipe-like cavities of a dark host rock called kimberlite. In South Africa diamonds are mined directly from the kimberlite. In Namibia and some other areas of Africa, diamonds are recovered from river beds of sand and rock where they have been released through erosion. More recently, diamonds have been extensively mined in Russia. Smaller deposits are in Brazil, India, and in the U.S. near Murfreesboro, Arkansas.

The Diamond Deva

"I ask you to live in Universal Truths that are given in the ethical principals of all religions. I ask you to honor all life as it has been created, and as it is being expressed in all life forms. The Universal Truths are infinite. When you live with respect and kindness for all others you will feel a continued connection with the Light of Truth. Knowing that you are always connected with the Light of Truth can give you the strength to act on the beliefs that you hold sacred, even when you are opposed by others. There are many who do not understand that the consequences of their selfish actions affect themselves and others even after they have left the Earth Plane. It is going to take your world a period of time before all will truly understand what I stand for.

"Those of you on the Earth Plane who are learning about the accumulation of material possessions have much to learn from me. To possess me you pay a high monetary price. You have an opportunity to learn that trying to possess anything only blocks you from creatively receiving life-force energy. Those of you who lack the monetary resources to purchase me are learning something as well. You are learning that you can be in a state of non-attachment to things and still receive from me as you read these words. There is a need for an energy flow coming in and going out of your lives. You are given time and space to utilize your material energies, and then you must release your mental connection with those energies, whether or not their physical presence is released. In this way you will learn the constant presence of the Light of Truth in the ebb and flow of physical form.''

Spiritual Aspects

Soul Tone: B
Chakra Affinities: Third Eye (1), Crown (1)
Subtle Body Affinities: Mental, Spiritual
Energy Focus: Building
Element: Air/Fire

Co-creating with Diamond

Diamond's physical hardness mirrors its spiritual quality of light-filled invincibility. Diamond purifies the will and encourages you to live according to a code of ethics which says to treat others as you would wish to be treated. You can take diamond when you need the courage to act on your spiritual and moral convictions. With fiery directness, diamond encourages honesty with self and others. You have to let down your defenses in order to find diamond's truth and light.

Alone, diamond works well on the third eye, and in combination with other stones diamond works best on the crown.

Affirmation

"I treat others as I would like to be treated."

EMERALD

Physical Aspects

Emerald is a brilliant green member of the beryl family, which also includes aquamarine. It is a beryllium aluminum silicate which gets its green color from the trace mineral chromium. Emerald is slightly harder than quartz at 8 on the Mohs' scale, and it has a trigonal crystalline structure. Emerald crystals are six-sided and sometimes striated in appearance. Emerald develops in pegmatites and certain metamorphic rocks. Gem-quality deposits are located in several areas of Colombia, where the emerald veins are loosened with sticks and the emeralds picked out by hand. Other deposits are located in Brazil, South Africa, and the U.S.

The Emerald Deva

"Through my energies you can experience the abundance of Unconditional Love and be healed by gratefully receiving that abundance. I can teach you about the larger meaning of prosperity. When you think that you are unworthy of any of the infinite forms of prosperity that are freely extended to you, you block the path of what you truly yearn for in this life. Anytime you increase your self-esteem or allow greater Light to enter your being, you are opening to prosperity. When you take care of your physical body, you are opening to prosperity. I know prosperity as energy that is always available, so one does not need to seek possession of it. When you try to "possess prosperity," it becomes elusive and passes between your fingers. You then become frustrated in your attempts to control or manipulate its energies. When you are feeling prosperous in a certain area of your life, are you at peace inside yourself at the same time? Or do you feel that you do not have enough? This thought form does not lead to fulfillment. Welcome the many forms of abundance in your life now and do not try to hold onto any one form of abundance. Understand that there is more than enough for all, and live with gratitude."

Spiritual Aspects

Soul Tone: F
Chakra Affinities: Heart (1), Third Eye (2)
Subtle Body Affinities: Emotional/Mental, Spiritual, Etheric
Energy Focus: Building
Element: Air

Co-creating with Emerald

The energies of emerald are uplifting and healing, for they connect you with your Source. Emerald can increase your awareness of abundance in other forms than purely monetary, and encourages gratitude when you are dealing with issues of financial support. It can also contribute to your sense of feeling supported by Higher Guidance. There are times when acknowledging our abundance brings just the healing that we need.

Affirmation

"I joyfully give thanks for the abundance in my life."

FIRE AGATE

Physical Aspects

Agate is a banded microcrystalline quartz or silicon dioxide in the trigonal system. Fire agate, in particular, comes in various shades of opaque brown with orange-red tints. The most important deposits for agates in general are in southern Brazil and northern Uruguay. Agates are often found with the other quartz minerals such as amethyst and carnelian. Fire agate is fairly common and can be found in a number of other locations as well.

The Fire Agate Deva

''Like fire, my energy can consume that which is no longer needed and move you forward with your focus on the larger picture. Lethargy is being in the state of idleness without a clear sense of connection to your energies and where they need to be focused in the next moment. Anything that remains in your energy system beyond its usefulness can create lethargy. My purpose is to clear that which you no longer need. My ultimate goal is to help you reconnect to your flow so that you have a sense of direction. Whether you experience my energies in a cathartic manner depends on you. When you are reconnected to your flow, there is greater space for new Unconditional Love to grow within you.''

Spiritual Aspects

Soul Tone: D
Chakra Affinities: Lower Abdomen (1), Root (2)
Subtle Body Affinities: Emotional/Mental, Etheric, Spiritual
Energy Focus: Clearing
Element: Fire/Earth

Co-creating with Fire Agate

Fire agate helps with *ambivalence*, whether it is lethargy relating to depression ("Monday morning blues") or wanting to remain in a space of the past. It strengthens physical vitality, cuts through sluggishness, and strengthens your will to focus on the present.

Affirmation

"I move forward with focus and direction and affirm that every moment is a new beginning."

FLUORITE

Physical Aspects

Fluorite is calcium fluoride that comes in a variety of colors, including violet, pale blue, green, yellow, and clear. It has a hardness of 4 and belongs to the isometric crystalline system. Crystals of fluorite are cubic or octahedral in shape, and you can commonly find them for sale in these forms. Because fluorite has perfect cleavage in all four directions, it can also easily be cut into octahedrons. Sometimes fluorite is radiated to give it a more even distribution of color, and it can also be synthesized. Fluorite will glow violet when exposed to ultraviolet rays, which can be an identifying characteristic. Large deposits of fluorite are found in England, West Germany, Ontario, and the midwestern U.S. We will discuss octahedral clear and purple fluorite.

The Clear Fluorite Deva

"I help you to accept your physical vehicle and your life on this Earth Plane as a spiritual teacher for

your growth. Whenever you feel limited by your physical state, I teach you to appreciate the present moment. When you wish you were somewhere else or
you desperately want something you don't have, I encourage you to work with the essentials that are at
hand. In this way I help you to quiet your will as well as
your conscious mind. When your will is quiet, you are
safe and protected, because there is nothing you need
and you can be in a state of fulfillment. This state of fulfillment can provide an expanded awareness which prepares you for further learning."

Clear Fluorite—Spiritual Aspects

Soul Tone: A# for the clearest stones; A for stones with a bluish
    tinge.
Chakra Affinities: Third Eye (1), Root (1), Crown (1)
Subtle Body Affinities: Emotional/Mental, Spiritual, Etheric
Energy Focus: Clearing, Building depending on how you focus
    your intention.
Element: Air

Co-creating with Clear Fluorite

When you desire something strongly which may not be for
your highest good, fluorite can help you release desire and focus
your attention on the present moment. If you are getting
caught in past memories and wishing for something that can no
longer be, fluorite "disconnects the line" so that you are free to
be in the here and now. Fluorite is helpful in meditation as you
empty your mind and will, and it gives a sense of "the void." If
you are feeling very disorganized, a few minutes with fluorite
can bring a sense of order, balance and stillness. You can hold
fluorite before you work with the pendulum, tarot, or other
tools with which you are seeking guidance. Fluorite can help
you release your own opinions in the matter. Clear octahedral
fluorite combines well with other stones in layouts.

Clear Fluorite Affirmation

"I release my personal will in order to purify my awareness."

The Purple Fluorite Deva

''You can only become aware of higher aspects of your being when your etheric, emotional, and mental subtle bodies are in harmony with the specific purpose of expanding your spiritual understanding. Sometimes when you release your personal will, a void is created. In this void space you can see more clearly what you are not, which can then prepare you for integrating Who You Are. My purple vibration can give you a more specific understanding of the deeper mysteries of life. Through the use of my form we travel to higher levels of spiritual awareness in order to change how you perceive your physical reality. You can sense that there is more to your life than your observable circumstances. Through my energies I help you move from the world of form into the world of formlessness, where time as you know it is infinite and limitless. I move you beyond the purity of awareness to an expanded state of understanding the foundation of existence.''

Purple Fluorite—Spiritual Aspects

Soul Tone: A, B (depending on your system of perception*)
Chakra Affinities: Third Eye (1)
Subtle Body Affinities: Emotional/Mental, Spiritual, Etheric
Energy Focus: Clearing, Building (depending on how you focus
     your intention)
Element: Air

Co-creating with Purple Fluorite

Purple fluorite is excellent for meditation because it prepares you by calming your desires and thoughts, and then takes you to higher levels of awareness. Its energies are very calming and peaceful, and it can move you beyond the space of pure

*Purple fluorite is one mineral in which it seems that the soul tone can be perceived through more than one perspective. Our experience is that the combination of belief, your intuitive manner of perceiving, and the level on which you are functioning on your spiritual path all determine how you perceive the soul tone.

awareness prepared by clear fluorite. It has less versatility in combination with other stones.

Purple Fluorite Affirmation

"As I merge with Divine Will I find greater peace and illumination."

GALENA

Physical Aspects

Galena is a heavy, gray lead sulphide with a hardness of 2½ and an isometric crystalline structure. Crystals are commonly found in the shapes of cubes and octahedrons. Galena is the most common of all lead minerals, and well-known deposits are found in Oklahoma, Kansas, and Missouri.

The Galena Deva

''I work more broadly with your energy system to help you provide the specific focus or center that is most appropriate for you at that moment. When you have been in a meditative state I can help you become more rooted in your physical body, so that you can integrate what you have learned on your spiritual journey. If your thoughts tend to scatter in many directions, or if you are feeling at loose ends emotionally, my focusing energy can help you establish your priorities.

''To effectively ground the energies that are being transmitted from outside your energy fields requires that I be able to harmonize with the entire spectrum of frequencies. Whereas clear quartz crystal works to expand your existing energies, my purpose is to align your energy field into your physical vehicle. You see, energies are stepped down as they move from higher to lower levels. To function in this capacity I need to match my energies to the predominant tone for each energy center.''

Spiritual Aspects

Soul Tone: All tones
Chakra Affinities: None
Subtle Body Affinities: Emotional/Mental, Etheric
Energy Focus: Building
Element: Earth

Co-creating with Galena

Galena does not have an affinity with a specific chakra. It can be held, utilized in meditation, or taken as an essence for any situation in which you need to settle, focus, or ground your energies. Galena can quiet your system before you go to bed, and is also useful if you feel spacy. It can also keep your thought-energies on a linear path when you are doing mental work. Galena can help a client calm extraneous thoughts before a session, and ground them after a session. You do not usually need an extended period of time with galena for centering to take place.

Affirmation

"I integrate my spiritual awareness by establishing my priorities and acting on them."

GARNET

Physical Aspects

The name garnet applies to a group of aluminum silicate minerals that differ mainly in the substitution of one mineral element in their compositions. All garnets have a hardness of 7–7½ and are isometric in their crystalline structure. Garnet crystals can occur in the form of dodecahedrons or trapezohedrons. The most well-known gem-quality garnet is pyrope garnet, which is an intense red, sometimes with shades or orange or brown. Gem-quality pyrope garnet comes from Arizona and Utah, as well as from Czechoslovakia and South Africa. Rhodolite is a variety of pyrope garnet that is rose red to pale violet and comes from North Carolina and Zaire.

Almandine garnet is deep red with violet tints. The stones are usually cut as cabochons with the back hollowed out so that they are thinner and therefore lighter in color. Garnets cut in this manner are called carbuncles. Almandine garnet is found in Alaska, Idaho, Brazil, and Australia. We have worked with the pyrope and rhodolite garnets.

The Garnet Deva

"There are times when you of the Human Kingdom need a tangible experience to recognize the strength that is present within you. My energies provide a tangible experience that can extend into your physical body and give the sense of life-force energies built up inside you. When you seek support for your efforts, I tell you to look within. My purpose is to guide you to that place within that can provide reassurance whenever you need it. Once you have felt this reservoir of energy within you, the opportunity to return to its source will always be present."

Spiritual Aspects

Soul Tone: C
Chakra Affinities: Root (1)
Subtle Body Affinities: Emotional/Mental, Etheric, Spiritual
Energy Focus: Building
Element: Earth

Co-creating with Garnet

If you are in a time of change or anxiety and feeling a little lost, garnet can provide a sense of rootedness which helps you focus practically on one step at a time. Garnet gives a sense of expanding strength in your capacity to reach a goal. Your protection is the affirmation of your own solid core. If you are inclined to rush around in too many directions and at too fast a pace, garnet can slow you down and help you prioritize your activities. Garnet will help you feel less depleted of vitality at the completion of your tasks.

Affirmation

"I affirm my reservoir of inner strength and I act with practicality."

IOLITE

Physical Aspects

Iolite is the gem trade name for translucent, blue and violet cordierite. Cordierite can also be brown or black, and is usually found in a massive or granular form, as crystals are very rare. Iolite is a magnesium aluminum silicate with a hardness of 7–7½ and an orthorhombic crystalline structure. Its colors can change from various shades of blue to gray as it is viewed from different directions. Iolite is generally associated with metamorphic rocks and mined in Burma and Brazil. Cordierite can be found in Connecticut and in various areas of the Northwest.

The Iolite Deva

''I link you directly into your *Soul* so that you can understand why you are here, and receive healing energy from lessons that you have already learned. The Soul is the composite energy memory of your being, which has no past, present or future, though past, present and future are contained within it. From your Higher Self you can receive specific guidance that is more ideally suited to the practical Earth Plane world. What is received from the Soul is the state of being where you live in Oneness. The Soul retains only the purest vibrations as you pass from one lifetime to another. The subconscious mind contains a record of areas where your Soul seeks to refine itself. Your Soul is therefore an integration of your purest qualities, perfectly balanced and ordered. It is through persistent intention that you can deepen your connection with your Soul.

''There are several ways you can work with me to access the energy of your Soul for healing. One is to first decide on a spiritual quality which you are trying to understand and master in your personal growth. Every spiritual quality has a specific frequency, and that frequency is then transmitted to you by your Soul. Another way is to ask your Soul to be present with you as you release what is no longer needed on your path. Your Soul then becomes a companion in your process, and you can be receptive to the qualities transmitted to you. I then guide you to integrate what you have received into your daily life.''

Spiritual Aspects

Soul Tone: B
Chakra Affinities: Third Eye (1), Crown (1)
Subtle Body Affinities: Spiritual
Energy Focus: Spiritual Expansion
Element: Air

Co-creating with Iolite

Connecting with your Soul through iolite is like *being* in a total state of Unconditional Love rather than merely thinking or feeling Unconditional Love. Iolite also gives a total sense of protection as you receive the energy you need. Take the essence as a preparation for a meditation in which you connect with your Soul. For a further discussion of how to work with iolite in meditation, see Part Three, Chapter 7. For healing, see the comments on iolite at the end of Chapter 8.

Affirmation

"I open to greater personal and spiritual growth through communication with my Soul."

JADE

Physical Aspects

The name jade is applied to two different opaque minerals, jadeite and neprite. They have similar characteristics and are very difficult to distinguish. Both types have a hardness of 6½–7 and they are very tough, which makes them ideal for carving. Jadeite and nephrite have a monoclinic crystalline structure. They come in many shades of green as well as black, red, brown, white, and green spotted with white.

Jadeite is rarer and is a sodium aluminum silicate. The most well-known deposits are in Burma, Guatemala, Japan, Mexico, and the U.S. Nephrite is found in China, Australia, Brazil, Canada, and Mexico. There are jade triplets on the market, and sometimes jade is dyed to make it a more emerald-like transparent green.

We refer to the nephrite jade below.

The Nephrite Jade Deva

''I promote the practice of detachment from the emotional body of the lifestream. I further encourage selective, focused thought. When you are seeking clarity in the mind I can help you release extraneous thoughts and emotions, so that you can maintain the discipline of being centered and balanced. My energies truly complement any spiritual practice.''

Spiritual Aspects

Soul Tone: E
Chakra Affinities: Solar Plexus (1), Heart (1), Third Eye (1)
Subtle Body Affinities: Emotional/Mental, Spiritual, Etheric
Energy Focus: Building, Clearing
Element: Earth/Air

Co-creating with Nephrite Jade

Jade's focused, calm balance is versatile in its effects. In past-life and dream work, jade moves slowly but deeply, and can help you detach from the emotions involved so that you can see more clearly. If you are emotionally oversensitive, jade can provide balance if used on an ongoing basis. It is also useful in mental work in which clear judgment and focus are important. Jade also can prepare you for meditation by calming and stilling your mind. It is an aid in promoting a more effortless discipline of any skill.

Affirmation

"My body, mind and spirit are in perfect balance."

KUNZITE

Physical Aspects

Kunzite is a pink-violet, gem-quality member of the spodumene family. It is a lithium aluminum silicate with a hardness of 6–7 and a monoclinic crystalline structure. Kunzite cleaves well in two directions, making it very sensitive to pressure and therefore difficult to cut. It has strong pleochroism, which means that it shows lighter and darker shades of pink-violet when viewed from different directions. Spodumene is found in pegmatite veins along with beryl and tourmaline, and it occasionally forms large crystals. Gem quality kunzite comes from California and Maine, and also from Brazil and Madagascar. We have also utilized clear kunzite, which might be more accurately called "clear spodumene."

The Lavender-pink Kunzite Deva

"In all things and in all ways, live your life to its fullest, both in the affairs of the physical plane and in the exploration of the Higher Spiritual Realms. Know that you are truly an unlimited being and there is no end to what you can create. The self-denial that has been practiced in the religions of your world has served its purpose in its time. However, self-denial has undertones of constriction that go beyond the process of purification. Whether you deny yourself certain things or hoard your physical possessions, the result is that energies are locked in place and are not free to move. I say that what is needed now is an expansion of life-force energies rather than a containment of their form. When you work with me you may feel "speeded up," because I dissolve any fears or hesitancy and I accelerate your willingness to enjoy and create new opportunities. When you expand your life-force energies by creating your life to the fullest, you benefit all life on this planet.

"Those of you who are attracted to me are opening your intuitive sensitivity and making a commitment to continue that unfoldment. When you listen to me through your inner sensitivity, I commit you to moderation as well as expansion so that your life-force energies are in balance as you accelerate your capacities. You will find that your energies are channeled into more activities that are filled with Light and Unconditional Love."

Lavender-pink Kunzite—Spiritual Aspects

Soul Tone: F
Chakra Affinities: Heart (1)
Subtle Body Affinities: Emotional/Mental, Spiritual, Etheric
Energy Focus: Building
Element: Water/Fire

Co-creating with Lavender-pink Kunzite

Kunzite can speed up a desire to create more beauty and fulfillment in your life. It heightens a desire to participate in activities in which you grow and receive in new ways. Kunzite also accelerates your creative potential and the desire to express that potential. you can work with it when you feel stuck or constricted in your self-expression. It will help you to understand the difference between moderation and constriction and will increase your enthusiasm and zest for life.

Lavender-pink Kunzite Affirmation

"I live my life zestfully and creatively to the fullest."

Clear Kunzite Deva

"Those of you who are drawn to my energies will choose the lavender-pink variety or the clear variety according to whether you will blend my energies at your heart and third eye, or work with me primarily at your third eye. I can teach you to expand the ways in which you work with your third eye energies. I can help you move beyond projecting energies and into higher frequencies where you work with life-force energies before they are created into solid physical substance. You are then learning about creativity at a higher level. You are truly unlimited in your ability to create."

Clear Kunzite—Spiritual Aspects

Soul Tone: A
Chakra Affinities: Third Eye (1)
Subtle Body Affinities: Emotional/Mental, Spiritual, Etheric
Energy Focus: Building
Element: Water/Fire

Co-creating with Clear Kunzite

The energies are similar in purpose to lavender-pink kunzite, except that they feel more active and perhaps focus more on understanding creativity in the spiritual realms. Our experience with both the lavender-pink and the clear kunzite is that it can stimulate the desire nature and also the desire to want everything *now*. When working with kunzite, ask about timing for pursuing your activities. Ask, "Is this the time for me to pursue _____ for my optimal balance?"

Clear Kunzite Affirmation

"I create to my highest capacity my vision of Light."

KYANITE

Physical Aspects

Kyanite is a translucent blue aluminum silicate. Along its axis the hardness if 4½, and perpendicular to its axis it is 6–7. Kyanite is a member of the triclinic crystalline family. Because of its variable hardness and its sensitivity to pressure, kyanite is difficult to cut. The crystals are shaped like long, flat blades with irregular streaks of differing shades of blue and brown. Kyanite is a metamorphic rock often found in gneiss and schist. The most striking blues come from Switzerland. Other deposits are located in North Carolina, Burma, Brazil, and Austria.

The Kyanite Deva

"I seek for you to become aware of how to work with finer levels of life-force energy for physical healing. When you hold my energies or internalize them, I take you to a level where you have a panoramic view of what your physical vehicle is really like, and where you can visually perceive its structure and sense its life-force energies. When your spiritual subtle body is activated, you can learn how to direct your energies so that they positively impact on the physical vehicle. With this knowledge you are encouraged to take appropriate action to restore the balance within. As you learn to better understand how the physical vehicle is an expression for spiritual perfection, your lifestyle will reflect a new balance. You will also work with the physical healing process in a more sensitive and finely tuned manner."

Spiritual Aspects

Soul Tone: A#
Chakra Affinities: Crown (1), Third Eye (1)
Subtle Body Affinities: Spiritual, Etheric
Energy Focus: Spiritual Expansion
Element: Air

Co-creating with Kyanite

Kyanite can aid you when you are dialoguing with your physical body in meditation. It affirms a sense of the Divinity and sacredness of the physical body, so that it can be easier to make healthy lifestyle changes. Kyanite's life-force energy can open the way for spiritual healing of the body if you work consciously with the idea that your body is a sacred temple and a manifestation of Love.

Affirmation

"My physical body is a sacred temple, built of pure love."

LABRADORITE

Physical Aspects

Labradorite is an opaque gray stone that shimmers with a metallic play of colors, especially greens and blues, when you hold it at certain angles. It was first discovered in the Canadian province of Labrador in 1770. Labradorite is a sodium calcium aluminum silicate member of the feldspar family. Like other feldspars it has a hardness of 6–6½ and a triclinic crystalline structure. The labradorite discovered in Finland in the early 1940s has a particularly wide variety of color and is sometimes sold under the trade name of "spectrolite." As well as Canada and Finland, labradorite is mined in the Malagasy Republic, Mexico, Russia, and the U.S.

The Labradorite Deva

''When you are reaching a crossroads in life, I can bring greater light to your decision making by helping you access the Akashic Records. The Akashic Records are the ultimate collection of all experiences from the very minute to the infinite. Experiences are stored as thought and feeling energy in the etheric forms of clear quartz crystal. Clear quartz crystal, as you know, has an infinite capacity to store energy. When you access the Akashic Records, you are an observer, receiving a pure picture of an experience, with its spiritual message as well as its physical, mental, or emotional content. In order to access the Akashic Records, your intent must be to apply the knowledge to your personal and spiritual growth. Otherwise the knowledge will not be made available to you.

''Both your subconscious mind and the Akashic Records are repositories of what has transpired through time. One difference is that your subconscious will carry information from more recent lifetime experiences. It is closer at hand and therefore more pertinent. You can also participate more fully in the details, beliefs, and feelings of the experience. With the Akashic Records you can go back to the very beginning of the existence. The scope of information is much broader. Accessing the Records can be helpful when you have accessed the subconscious mind and there is a sense that something more is needed.

"When working with the Akashic Records, you might ask to be shown when you exhibited specific spiritual qualities and manifested them in their highest order and form. You can then ask that they be connected into your energy system so that they can be applied in your present life. If you have had difficulties with a particular person, you might ask to see what has transpired, and how the optimal healing can be achieved. This can be like a past-life experience, but you observe it more impersonally and you receive a broader panoramic overview of the spiritual lessons involved. You can also ask to be shown what a particular situation could look like when the blocks are totally removed from the experience. The changes indicated could involve action or a change in belief or perception about the experience.

"You can refer to me as the timeless teacher, for I can take you on a journey into what was, what is, and what can be."

Spiritual Aspects

Soul Tone: B
Chakra Affinities: Third Eye (1), Crown (1)
Subtle Body Affinities: Spiritual
Energy Focus: Spiritual expansion
Element: Air

Co-creating with Labradorite

Utilize the essence or the stone for a meditation to access the Akashic Records (see Part III, Chapter 10, for comments on meditation). With labradorite you can inquire about the past to support your present. You can also ask to receive information that is related to your spiritual purpose.

Affirmation

"I now access the Akashic Records in order to expand my spiritual growth."

LAPIS LAZULI

Physical Aspects

Lapis lazuli, or lapis for short, is actually an opaque conglomerate of dark blue lazurite streaked with white calcite, or sprinkled with gold specks of pyrite. Lapis may also include small quantities of augite, diopside, mica, and hornblende. This mixture is found when sodium, aluminum, and calcium combine but lack sufficient silica to form a feldspar. Lapis belongs to the isometric crystalline system and has a hardness of 5–6.

The finest lapis, with an intense, uniform blue, comes from Afghanistan. One of the ways that it is mined is to light a fire on the host limestone rock, which is then put out with water. The sudden change in temperature weakens the limestone rocks, which can then be broken away with hammers. The pockets of lapis can then be lifted out with crowbars. Lapis is also found in Siberia and Chile. The color of Chilean lapis is less intense and has larger streaks of white calcite. Lapis has been found in this country in Colorado and California. Swiss lapis is an imitation stone made from staining jasper with a Prussian blue dye.

The Lapis Lazuli Deva

"I penetrate thought energy which may seem 'rational' but is in truth non-essential, so that you can see clearly what may actively be affecting your energy system. I encourage your presence with me in this process so that you can become more focused in your mind. Whenever you seek to clear anything that is stored within your subconscious mind, I ask you to formulate a question that relates to what is occuring in the present moment. I utilize this energy pattern to pinpoint the area of the subconscious where its energy counterpart is stored. Throughout this process, I emphasize 'clear sight.' I help you then to move into a space where you initiate action to make the changes that need to be made.''

Spiritual Aspects

Soul Tone: G#, A   Stones with more white calcite may test G#
   and deeper blue lapis tests A.
Chakra Affinities: Third Eye (1)
Subtle Body Affinities: Mental, Spiritual
Energy Focus: Clearing, Building
Element: Fire/Earth

Co-creating with Lapis Lazuli

With its steady, penetrating energy, lapis helps you look at things you have been avoiding. Spiritually, it strengthens the desire for truth. When you are ill and don't know why, lapis is one of the stones that can help you become aware of the issues. Lapis essence can be taken before past-life work or for spiritual purification. Lapis with more white calcite is calmer and steadier in its energies, while lapis with more pyrite gives fiery overtones.

Affirmation

   "I seek the truth in understanding my experiences."

LARIMAR

Physical Aspects

Larimar is the trade name for gem quality blue pectolite. Pectolite comes in other colors, including clear, white, green, and pink. It is a sodium calcium silicate with a hardness of 4½–5 and a triclinic crystalline structure. The beautiful blue of larimar comes from traces of copper. Pectolite is not generally considered to be gem material because it is normally found as a loose aggregate not cohesive enough to cut. However, larimar has more compact fibers and can take a high polish, which sometimes gives a cat's-eye effect (an effect resembling the slit eye of a cat caused by the reflection of light by parallel fibers). Larimar is considered rare, because it is found only in the Dominican Republic. Other colors of pectolite are found in Scotland, Sweden, Canada, Alaska, and Arkansas.

We have worked with a larimar that is a robin's-egg blue.

The Larimar Deva

"Deep inside many of you there is a yearning to express your greater spiritual service in a more original, diverse manner. My energies act as a catalyst to bring this energy and awareness into your consciousness, where you can then move with it. I encourage a pioneering spirit. Welcome unusual insights, and seek to express them without desire for recognition. Do not be concerned if what you say is not understood by those around you, for you truly may be working from a different level. Perhaps you are ahead of your time. What I bring is strength and reassurance that you are truly on your path, when you sense yourself as separated from the masses. Do not seek recognition from others. Your recognition comes from the greater service that you give. It is an inner sense of fulfilling your spiritual purpose. You are learning how unlimited you truly are.

"You ask me why I am relatively rare. I say to you that as more and more lifestreams seek to express from their higher spiritual service, those that are in need of my energies will indeed find me."

Spiritual Aspects

Soul Tone: G
Chakra Affinities: Throat (1)
Subtle Body Affinities: Emotional/Mental, Spiritual, Etheric
Energy Focus: Building
Element: Fire

Co-creating with Larimar

Larimar can be useful as a confidence builder when you are involved in an ongoing spiritual service project which involves doing something in a new way. Examples would be starting a unique service that helps people in some manner, or experimenting with a way to conserve a natural resource. Larimar helps you to move out of conventional ways of thinking and doing things so that you are free to dream up innovative possibilities. Larimar can be excellent for brainstorming, when you need to come up with ways to manifest a particular service that has been in the back of your mind for a long time. Larimar's energies strengthen your desire to express a unique service, rather than simply expanding your mental creativity.

Affirmation

"I fulfill my spiritual service in a way that is uniquely my own, in order to help others understand the unlimited nature of growth and knowledge."

MAGNETITE

Physical Aspects

Magnetite is a metallic, black iron oxide with a hardness of 5½–6½ and an isometric crystalline structure. It is one of the most abundant of all the oxide minerals and occurs in a variety of environments. A distinguishing physical characteristic is its magnetic property.

The Magnetite Deva

"You have come to Planet Earth for infinite reasons. Your main purpose for being here is to grow and expand your spiritual awareness. I urge you to commit your total being to this process. Whenever you are having second thoughts about moving forward on your spiritual path, my energies can give you the needed push to go forward once again. Sometimes you may not truly comprehend why I am stimulating inner movement toward a particular outer manifestation. As your path continues to unfold, you will see why you were guided to move in a particular direction."

Spiritual Aspects

Soul Tone: C#
Chakra Affinities: Root (1)
Subtle Body Affinities: Emotional/Mental, Etheric
Energy Focus: Clearing, Building
Element: Water

Co-creating with Magnetite

Magnetite gently but directly propels you toward change. It gives a sense that change is inevitable and that it is something to which you can look forward. If you are reluctant or fearful about leaving a situation behind that seems familiar and secure, magnetite helps you to grow in a new way. If you have felt a sense of agitation or depression from people or a place, magnetite can give protection and aid you in releasing those feelings.

Affirmation

"I trust my abilities to accelerate change."

MALACHITE

Physical Aspects

Malachite is a layered green, opaque stone of the monoclinic system. It is a basic copper carbonate containing eight percent water with a hardness of 3½–4. Because it is a secondary copper mineral, it is often found with other copper carbonates such as azurite. The finest malachite comes from the Urals in Russia, Chile, Zaire, South Africa, and in this country, from Arizona. Malachite polishes to a silky luster, which has made it a popular choice for jewelry. It is sensitive to heat, acids, ammonia, and hot water. Malachite will lose its sheen if you soak it in salt water. You can clean it with salt or with some other method.

The Malachite Deva

"Fear that appears as part of your experiences is not to be considered a sign of weakness, as you may have been taught. I see an initial step in uprooting fear from your being. That step is to understand why the fear has surfaced in the first place. When you understand the nature of this fear, it is unlikely to resurface, once its imbalance has been removed from the energy field. Fear can be very tenacious and stubborn, so more intensified energies are well suited for accomplishing this order of service to the Human Kingdom. When you feel immobilized by fear, I give you courage and strengthen your resolve to be more than you thought you could be."

Spiritual Aspects

Soul Tone: E or F, depending on the individual stone.
Chakra Affinities: Solar Plexus (1), Heart (1), Lower Abdomen (2)
Subtle Body Affinities: Emotional/Mental, Etheric, Spiritual
Energy Focus: Clearing
Element: Fire/Earth

Co-creating with Malachite

Malachite, with its intense probing action, can help you break free from limitations related to fear, guilt, or self-denial. It increases both determination and courage in any situation because it helps dissolve acute fear and anxiety. Malachite is an invaluable aid when you are working on the release of old, limiting habit patterns.

Affirmation

"I have the courage and determination to work through all fear."

MOLDAVITE

Physical Aspects

Moldavite is a trade name for green tektite. Tektites are meteorite "glass" fragments that range from a million to a billion years old. They vary in size from microscopic to the size of an orange. Chemically, tektites are silicon dioxide plus aluminum oxide. They register 5½ on the hardness scale and have an amorphous crystalline structure. This amorphous structure, with its large bubbles and swirls, suggests that their shape and size is due to rapid heating followed by cooling upon entry into our atmosphere. Tektites are normally brown and black in color; the translucent green moldavites are found only in Czechoslovakia. Moldavite is rare and therefore more expensive than many stones.

The Moldavite Deva

"My purpose is twofold. The first purpose is to expand your understanding of who you are in relationship to the universe. Second is to be a vehicle for you to enter into other dimensions of reality for a greater understanding of life. The quality of my energy has a releasing effect, so that when you understand your true nature, you can move out of limited thinking to a greater knowledge of Self. Let me give you an example to explain what I am saying. You are told that you must limit certain physical activities, and you have accepted that viewpoint as being totally true for you. My energies enlarge your perception of who you are, so that you can choose to renew your efforts to pursue these activities, or you can choose to no longer feel limited by your circumstances.

"In addition to bringing awareness of the Greater Light within yourself so that you can expand beyond limited personal thinking, I can help you connect to the infinite wisdom that lies outside your being. All forms of life are interconnected, and you have the capacity to communicate with the intelligence on other planets and stars, where time no longer exists as you know it.

"The process of interdimensional communication works in the following manner. Signals are sent as energy from your Higher Self mind into interdimensional space and are received by Light Beings who have refined the spiritual tool of telepathic thought transference. The nature of your contact is perceived and moves through channels until the right spiritual entity is found to answer your inquiry. Once the channels are connected between the spiritual entity and your Higher Self mind, then the process of communication can begin. Sometimes your Higher Self may be able to channel this knowledge directly into your conscious mind. Whether this is done instantaneously or in a selected space of time is in direct relationship to the openness and receptivity of your conscious mind. Just as patience is a significant lesson that you are learning while living on the Earth Plane, patience is required by anyone seeking to establish contact with Light Beings in other dimensions. A prerequisite is to let go of any comparisons between yourself and any other Light Being. Remember that the process of learning and growth is taking place in other realities as well. Remember to communicate a pure sense of thankfulness to the Light Being with whom you share time and space in this process. Unconditional Love knows no bonds and is thus a cosmic, universal concept in all dimensions. Utilize the quality of Light in all forms of communication with Light Beings.

"Two things are achieved by seeking to expand to other dimensional levels. First, there is an understanding that there are other lifestreams with the capacity to assist you and your Planet in its evolutionary cycle. Second, there is an activation that takes place within your own mind that helps you to create more solutions to

the imbalance currently on your Planet. I work co-creatively in this capacity with clear quartz crystal. The goal,
you see, is to expand your access to greater knowing.''

Spiritual Aspects

Soul Tone: B   Will respond to F if the stone is put on the thy-
    mus gland.
Chakra Affinities: Thymus Gland (1), Third Eye (1), Crown (1)
Subtle Body Affinities: Spiritual, Etheric, Emotional/Mental
Energy Focus: Spiritual Expansion, Clearing
Element: Air

Co-creating with Moldavite

If you feel "out of touch" with your spiritual connection, or
you feel that your life is currently without spiritual meaning,
moldavite can reconnect you spiritually. This reconnection will
most likely involve change and regeneration, giving you an opportunity to drop limiting beliefs that are keeping you from
receiving greater spiritual awareness.

You can also work with moldavite at your third eye and
crown in meditation for interdimensional communications (see
Chapter 10).

Moldavite Affirmation

"I go beyond limited thinking and receive the Unconditional Love present in other dimensions of the Universe."

MOONSTONE

Physical Aspects

Moonstone is a potassium aluminum silicate member of the
feldspar family. It is a translucent, milky white stone with a hardness of 6–6½ and a monoclinic crystalline structure. Its shimmering effect is caused by the alternating layers of orthoclase
and albite feldspars. When these layers are thin and you hold a
moonstone up to reflected light, you will see a beautiful blue-

white glimmer. Moonstone is mined in Sri Lanka, Australia, Brazil, and the U.S.

The Moonstone Deva

"I see the emotional body as holding the key to maintaining balance and wellness throughout your being. Each feeling you have passes through several stages before it has an impact on your physical vehicle. First the feeling becomes a presence that you may or may not be totally aware of. Second, as you become aware of your feelings, you examine them without acting on them. Third, you decide how you are going to respond to their presence.

"The quality of your action depends on the acceptance of your feelings. If you feed life-force energy to a feeling of anger or sadness, your actions will carry the imbalanced energy. When this happens, the process of integrating the results of your actions takes more persistence and patience. I tell you through my energies that I love you unconditionally and that I understand the sensitive feeling space that you are in at the moment. I encourage an acceptance of what you are feeling so that you can then gently release the need for that experience. Accept yourself as you are, and know that you can creatively change yourself, not because of some external experience, but because it feels more right and peaceful inside of you to do so."

Spiritual Aspects

Soul Tone: G#, A, depending on the individual stone.
Chakra Affinities: Third Eye (1), Solar Plexus (1)
Subtle Body Affinities: Emotional/Mental, Etheric, Spiritual
Energy Focus: Clearing, Building
Element: Water

Co-creating with Moonstone

Moonstone can help you accept what you are feeling when you need to release emotional tension. It has a calm, flowing peace that helps restore emotional balance in everyday experiences, such as worry or overreaction to a situation. Moonstone can help you better understand dreams that are telling you about your emotional state of balance. With moonstone you may also respond more sensitively to the emotional nature of others.

Affirmation

"I value my emotional sensitivity, knowing that it is all right to feel what I am feeling."

MOSS AGATE

Physical Aspects

Moss agate is a clear micrcrystalline quartz with moss-green inclusions of hornblende. Scientifically it is not considered an agate because it is not layered. Like other quartz, it is silicon dioxide with a hardness of 7 and a trigonal crystalline structure. The best gem qualities come from India, and it is also found in China and the U.S.

The Moss Agate Deva

''My energies help you to attune to the Spiritual Consciousness in all forms of life found within the Kingdoms of Nature. I help you understand that opening to the world of spirit means receiving the Unconditional Love that is Consciousness. As you expand spiritually, the connection between your self-identity and your Higher Self becomes closer and more pure than ever before. My energies reassure you of this process so that you can take steps forward to bring about its completion within you. If you find that you have reached a certain plateau in your growth and there is a sense of fear about moving to another level of understanding, I can give you reassurance and trust so that the unknown is not traumatic. When you can replace your fear of the unknown with Unconditional Love, the flow of life-force energy into your body is increased. You must initiate action to understand the Spiritual Dimension of all physical reality. Once you make that commitment, I can lay the groundwork in your subtle bodies for your spiritual expansion.''

Spiritual Aspects

Soul Tone: E
Chakra Affinities: Thymus Gland (1), Solar Plexus (1)
Subtle Body Affinities: Spiritual, Etheric, Emotional/Mental
Energy Focus: Spiritual Expansion
Element: Air

Co-creating with Moss Agate

Moss agate can be a bridge for connecting with your Higher Self and the Kingdoms of Nature, because it can increase the flow of Unconditional Love into your subtle bodies. It can be placed on the solar plexus or thymus gland to aid you in receiving additional life-force energies for healing and well-being. The essence can be taken before a meditation or a walk in the woods, to prepare you and help you release fears of the unknown. You can also try moss agate when you are working to heal your "inner child." The spiritual opening it gives can allow for the infusion of Unconditional Love, which in turn strengthens your self-identity and connection with your Higher Self.

Affirmation

"I find the God/Goddess/All That Is in all of life."

OBSIDIAN

Physical Aspects

Obsidian is formed when silica-rich volcanic magma flows onto the Earth's surface and rapidly solidifies into an amorphous glassy solid. It is generally black, although sometimes it is mixed with brown and called mahogany obsidian, or white, which we call snowflake obsidian. As a natural glass, obsidian has a hardness of 5–5½. We have utilized snowflake and mahogany obsidian.

The Obsidian Deva

"My purpose is to uproot those energies from within your being that you no longer need. I am well suited to do this kind of work with the Human Kingdom, since I am created through volcanic activity. When I have completed my work with you, there may be a heightened sense of vulnerability inside. You may experience a void in the space where imbalanced energies have been removed. Whatever sensations you may experience during my work, be reassured that the process you have undergone will allow more light to be present within. Sometimes you may experience flashbacks from your experience with me. Know, however, that if they do happen, they will be temporary in nature. When greater opportunities for spiritual growth of the Soul are present in your conscious awareness, then my purpose in your life is complete."

Spiritual Aspects

Soul Tone: Mahogany obsidian, C, snowflake obsidian, C#
Chakra Affinities: Root (1), Lower Abdomen (1), Solar Plexus (2)
Subtle Body Affinities: Emotional/Mental, Etheric, Spiritual
Energy Focus: Clearing
Element: Fire

Co-creating with Obsidian

The different kinds of obsidian have varying intensities, and we have found the snowflake and mahogany obsidians to provide more continuity in energy flow. Obsidian performs a task similar to dream imagery. In a dream the characters may at times exaggerate self-effacement, stubbornness, anger, etc. Your subconscious may paint these ludicrous pictures in order to attract your attention to the problem at hand. Obsidian can also amplify our negative emotions and thoughts so that we are more aware of them. Meditating on volcanoes will give you a feel for how obsidian may work with your energies. If you tend toward cynicism or rebelliousness on a particular subject, obsidian can abruptly cut through a hard outer shell. It can also be useful in a situation where you have been stubbornly fighting the process of looking within. Obsidian also helps release anger and can activate a positive sense of power that moves you to take charge of your situation. Obsidian can also be utilized to release subconscious memories that affect the lower three chakras.

Working with obsidian can have an irritating effect on your energy fields, so it is wise to be certain that obsidian is the mineral you need at a given time. It is best to work with the volcanic energies of obsidian with focused thoughts. Questions you might ask are, "What attitudes about myself do I need to change?" Or, "What attitudes or experiences do I need to be aware of in order to clear them?" Once you have become more aware, change your focus to, "What qualities do I need to affirm in myself?"

Affirmation

"Letting go of my resistance to looking inward frees my personal power to bring about change."

OPAL

Physical Aspects

Opal is a hydrous silicon dioxide with a hardness of 5½–6½. There are three main groupings of opal: precious opal, fire opal, and common opal. Precious opal is transparent to translucent and has a rainbow-like iridescence which changes as you look at it from different angles. Originally, opal was classified in the amorphous category of crystalline structures, and the iridescence was thought to be due to the refraction of light on its thin surface layers. In the 1960s observations with an electron microscope revealed that opal is a very orderly structure of tiny spheres of the mineral cristobalite, layered in siliceous "jelly." The distance between these spheres is approximately the same length as the wavelength of light, so that diffraction occurs when the light hits the stone, causing the irridescence.

Sometimes opal is cut very thin and mounted as a doublet on another backing in order to bring out the colors. Opal has also been made synthetically, and there are several ways of livening up the color with artificial resins and dyes. Precious opal is classified as white or black opal, depending on whether the color flashes are in a white or dark background.

Opal contains water, and sometimes when it loses water, the opalescence diminishes. It can be restored by storing it in damp cotton wool.

Fire opal is named for its reddish-orange color. It does not have the rainbow iridescence and can be transparent to translucent. Glass imitations are on the market. Mexico is an excellent source for gem-quality fire opals.

White opal is mostly opaque and is also without the play of color. It looks like milky quartz but is softer and breaks differently. It is formed at a lower temperature than quartz and develops in a wide variety of rocks as a cavity filling. Common opal is widespread and easily obtainable.

The most well-known precious opal deposits are in Australia, Brazil, Japan, and the western U.S. We have worked with the inexpensive common opal and the precious opal.

The Opal Deva

"I am a bold and dynamic disperser of Light, and I can clear beliefs that limit your freedom and independence. I sense the importance of starting fresh and I help you initiate new ways of thinking and a more spontaneous approach to life. Because of my internal structure, I have the ability to express from a broader spectrum of color frequencies. Like you, I do not wish to be 'possessed.' I encourage freedom at all levels and help you build your own unique and positive Light space. My energies unlock the creative channels within you that are a part of your unique contribution to others."

Spiritual Aspects

Soul Tone: A
Chakra Affinities: Third Eye (1)
Subtle Body Affinities: Emotional/Mental, Spiritual, Etheric
Energy Focus: Clearing, Building
Element: Fire

Co-creating with Opal

Opal, with its expanding intensity, encourages both freedom and independence. Its energy can feel like firecrackers on the Fourth of July, or like a sunburst of energy. Opal can help you answer the question, "What blocks me from fully expressing myself?" It is a good stone for expanding creativity. Opal can also help you release anger and claim your self-worth. Opal also aids in locating and dissolving past-life memories.

Affirmation

"I am now free and independent, as I expand beyond perceived limitations from my past."

PEARL

Physical Aspects

Pearls are not classified as minerals, because they are organic in origin. They are formed by two particular species of shellfish called pearl mollusks and pearl oysters as an immune defense against irritants such as parasites. When a parasite enters the fleshy part of the mollusk, the animal surrounds it with a secreted substance called mother-of-pearl or nacre. Mother-of-pearl is calcium carbonate (84–92%) cemented together with an organic substance called conchiolin (4–13%). Mother-of-pearl can be pink, silver, cream, golden, green, or blue. It is the substance produced by the mantle of the mollusk that lines its inner shell.

The finest natural pearls are called oriental pearls, and they come from the Persian Gulf, off the coast of southern India, and Australia. Freshwater pearls are found in the rivers of the Mississippi Valley.

The increased demand for pearls has led to their cultivation, particularly in Japan. Today cultured pearls make up about ninety percent of the total trade. Cultured pearls are made by inserting a rounded mother-of-pearl bead, along with a piece of tissue from the mantle of a pearl mollusk, into another pearl mollusk. Natural pearls and cultured pearl are very similar in appearance, and cultured pearls must be designated as such.

We have worked with mother-of-pearl, in the form of a small polished stone, which comes from the mantle or inner lining of the shell.

The Pearl Deva

''My energies gently encourage you to look at those things that are upsetting you emotionally. Sometimes your emotions need to be agitated to help you see what you need to release. My work is best done with those whose sensitivity to their emotional nature is finely tuned. Although I can help you access past lives, I am best utilized in helping you release and balance the experiences of this present life.

''Many of you live life constantly surrounded by a protective outer shell that you have created. Sometimes you need the nurturing of emotional detachment from a situation. Sometimes you need to risk yourself in a situation that feels like a sacrifice, in order to be able to receive at a later time. The sacrifice is that of becoming more vulnerable and sensitive to your outer world. You acquire wisdom in learning to move back and forth from emotional detachment and emotional risk.

''My physical function as a protector shows one side of reality, and my spiritual quality as a catalyst to encourage emotional risk shows another side. In each way I serve a teaching function, so that you have a complete picture. When you can integrate emotional protection with vulnerability, you will have balance.''

Spiritual Aspects

Soul Tone: A
Chakra Affinities: Third Eye (1), Heart (2)
Subtle Body Affinities: Emotional/Mental, Spiritual, Etheric
Energy Focus: Clearing
Element: Water

Co-creating with Pearl

Once you have started a release process of some kind, pearl brings a sense of inner strength, emotional peace, and a nurturing space for you to complete your work. Pearl essence can be helpful in a personal or counseling situation to encourage emotional risk. You can work with it also for emotional protection.

Affirmation

"As I risk myself emotionally in order to heal, I am protected and nurtured."

PERIDOT

Physical Aspects

Peridot, or olivine, as it is sometimes called, is a transparent, yellow-green magnesium iron silicate. Its unique green is due to the iron and traces of nickel in its content. Peridot's hardness is 6½–7 and it has an orthorhombic crystalline structure. The most well-known deposit is on St. John's Island on the Red Sea, where it has been mined for 3,500 years. Peridot is also found in Burma, South Africa, Brazil, Mexico, and Arizona.

The Peridot Deva

"Jade says happiness is a *state of being*. I say that happiness is an *expression of being*. My purpose is to give you joy, so that you can spontaneously spread my Light to all other lifestreams. When you are feeling 'joy-full' and sunny, you can see the Sun in others. I encourage you to keep the life-force energies flowing by expressing your delight. Take time to give to others, and tell them how much you appreciate their work and their gifts of service."

Spiritual Aspects

Soul Tone: E
Chakra Affinities: Heart (1), Solar Plexus (1)
Subtle Body Affinities: Emotional/Mental, Spiritual, Etheric
Energy Focus: Building
Element: Fire

Co-creating with Peridot

Peridot revitalizes the sense of inner joy that shines like the sun. It encourages you to express that joy to others. Peridot opens you to giving and receiving. When you dislike certain aspects of your daily life, peridot can give you an optimism that helps you delight in little things. Peridot also encourages an extroverted expresson of appreciation of others in order to keep you from taking others for granted. It helps you feel a confident joy that you have something to give, and reminds you how beautiful you are and how beautiful the world is.

Affirmation

"Inner joy lights my way, and I share that joy with others."

PYRITE

Physical Aspects

Pyrite is the stone that is commonly called "fool's gold." It is an iron disulphide with a hardness of 6–6½ and an isometric crystalline structure. The crystals occur predominantly in cubes but can assume other geometric shapes as well. Pyrite is the most widespread and abundant of the sulphide minerals and can be found in a number of places in the U.S. Pyrites that can be cut are mined in Italy.

The Pyrite Deva

"My energies help provide a base of life-force energies that can be utilized throughout your physical vehicle. I see myself as an energy channel, since I function as a transmitter of life-force energies that are continually being received from the Sun and the core energy of Planet Earth herself. Inertia takes place when there is insufficient energy present to generate movement. This can occur at any level of your being. I often hear lifestreams express, 'I really don't want to think about this,' or 'I am too tired and worn out to make a change.' Yes, I see an emotional and mental aspect to this situation. However, I work by adding greater life-force energy to the system. The integration of additional life-force energy and a change in thinking is a key for the return of normal energy flow."

Spiritual Aspects

Soul Tone: C
Chakra Affinities: Root (1), Base of Spine (1)
Subtle Body Affinities: All
Energy Focus: Building
Element: Fire

Co-creating with Pyrite

Pyrite does not give specific emotional or mental qualities. Rather, it is a more generalized energy builder, as clear quartz crystal can be. When you need energy on any level, place pyrite at the root or base of the spine and affirm that you are receiving an energy boost. You can follow pyrite with other stones, which may then have a more powerful effect because they will have more energy to realign. If you take the essence you may feel a more diffused, overall "spread" of energy that can revitalize you on whatever level you need.

Affirmation

"I open to receive additional life-force energy wherever it is needed."

RHODOCHROSITE

Physical Aspects

Rhodochrosite is an opaque manganese carbonate that is concentrically banded in layers of rose and white. It has a hardness of 4 and belongs to the trigonal system. There are several large deposits in Argentina, as well as in Romania and Colorado.

The Rhodochrosite Deva

''I teach you about loving yourself unconditionally. When you find it difficult to forgive and accept yourself and others, you can feel lonely and separated from the life-force energies of Unconditional Love. I help you to develop a compassionate heart. I do not mean a 'bleeding heart,' where you take the burdens of others upon yourself. Rather, it is listening to yourself and others with sensitive ears and letting your responses be channeled with Unconditional Purity and Love.

''My energies work effectively for the release of pain and deep hurt that you may have stored within your heart. Self-acceptance releases pain. Mistakes really are gifts that allow us to bring ourselves in alignment with Divine Harmony. Always focus on the beauty of who you are, rather than the imperfection of what you are not.''

Spiritual Aspects

Soul Tone: F
Chakra Affinities: Heart (1), Solar Plexus (2)
Subtle Body Affinities: Emotional/Mental, Etheric, Spiritual
Energy Focus: Clearing, Building
Element: Fire/Water

Co-creating with Rhodochrosite

Renewal is a key quality for rhodochrosite. There is a fiery intensity that strengthens the initiative to begin again after pain. There is also a watery, gentler compassion that brings self-acceptance. Rhodochrosite can help ease the loneliness that comes from feeling "not good enough." As a heart opener, rhodochrosite can dissolve anger and self-criticism; therefore it is a catalyst for forgiveness of self and others.

Affirmation

"I accept that I am truly a lovable being, and I forgive those who have forgotten that they are loved."

RHODONITE

Physical Aspects

Rhodonite is a light rose to flesh pink stone with black veins and inclusions of manganese oxide. It is a manganese silicate with a hardness of 5½–6½ and a triclinic crystalline structure. Rhodonite forms in metamorphic rocks and is mined in Sweden, Australia, the U.S., and Canada.

The Rhodonite Deva

"Sometimes I sense within you a deep longing to keep the past. When you hold onto possessions or memories of the past, you draw comparisons with the present. You develop expectations that seem to fall short of what you enjoyed 'back then,' and you experience only fleeting happiness. My energies help you allow the past to rest as a treasured memory, without a need to resurrect it in the present moment. Whenever you have to release something on the Earth Plane, there is often a sense of loss, and I bring you a sense of empathy and healing. I help you understand that you cannot live through your past while seeking to grow in the present."

Spiritual Aspects

Soul Tone: D#
Chakra Affinities: Lower Abdomen (1), Solar Plexus (1)
Subtle Body Affinities: Emotional/Mental, Etheric
Energy Focus: Clearing
Element: Water/Earth

Co-creating with Rhodonite

Rhodonite encourages you to get on with your daily life and forget looking back at the past. Therefore, it is useful when you get caught in nostalgic memories and cloud the present with unrealistic expectations or lack of focus. Rhodonite helps you release your hold on what was and accept what is in the present. It can heighten an interest in daily affairs.

Affirmation

"I release my longing for the past as I find in every day something beautiful and new for me to appreciate."

ROSE QUARTZ

Physical Aspects

Rose quartz is a translucent pink silicon dioxide with a hardness of 7 and a trigonal crystalline structure. The rose color comes from the trace mineral titanium. Crystals with flat faces are rare and have only been found within the past few years. Brazil and the Malagasy Republic have large deposits of rose quartz.

The Rose Quartz Deva

''I help you to live this life as fully as you can, and to find pleasure in all of life around you. I also help you to move from a place of being hard-hearted to a gentle place of being more 'flexible-hearted.' I fooled you. You thought I was going to say 'soft-hearted.' Some people think that to be soft-hearted is to be weak. To me being soft-hearted is to learn about the power of your emotions and how your emotions can create a positive flow of life-force energy. When you are enjoying beauty, the flow of softness and delight in your heart creates a positive energy of Unconditional Love in yourself and others.''

Spiritual Aspects

Soul Tone: F
Chakra Affinities: Heart (1)
Subtle Body Affinities: Emotional/Mental, Etheric, Spiritual
Energy Focus: Building
Element: Water

Co-creating with Rose Quartz

Rose quartz builds self-confidence and self-acceptance by asking you to give pleasure to yourself and to smile. It encourages you to slow down, be more light-hearted, and make time in your life for joy and delight. Rose quartz can also heighten your awareness of the beauty around you in order to dissolve gloom, despondency, and over-seriousness.

Affirmation

"I delight in play and pleasure."

RUBY

Physical Aspects

Ruby is the trade name for red corundum. It is an aluminum oxide with a hardness of 9 and a trigonal crystalline structure. Ruby can range in color from rose to a dark purplish red. It gets color from traces of chrome. As a rough stone, ruby looks dull, but when cut its luster is like diamond. Inclusions of rutile in a cut ruby can look like a six-pointed star; this is called star ruby. Because ruby is comparatively heavy, it is mined by panning and then picking out the rubies by hand. Important deposits are in Burma and Sri Lanka. Rubies are also found in North Carolina. There are many imitations on the market in the form of doublets, triplets, and synthetic rubies.

The Ruby Deva

"My guiding purpose is to help you evolve into a greater expresson of your true Self and Spiritual Nature. When you are being your true Divine Essence, you are in a space to give Unconditional Love to others, as well as to Nature. It takes courage to refrain from judging another lifestream and to follow your intuitive sensitivity rather than your logical mind. It takes courage to take on the role of leadership when others have become disconnected from the group focus. My energies can strengthen you in these kinds of experiences, so that the expression of your will is purified through the Unconditional Love of your Heart. As you radiate this state of being, know that you are creating positive life-force energies for the personal and spiritual growth of others.''

Spiritual Aspects

Soul Tone: F#   Lighter rubies may test F, darker rubies may test F#.
Chakra Affinities: Heart (1), Root (1)
Subtle Body Affinities: Emotional/Mental, Spiritual, Etheric
Energy Focus: Building
Element: Fire

Co-creating with Ruby

Ruby's fiery energy builds confidence by strengthening your courage and will to be who you are. It is helpful against self-dislike and can give you an energy boost when you are doing something you have never done before. When you need to move into a leadership role, ruby can give you the confidence to make decisions that others may not like. Ruby's intensity will keep you moving in your chosen direction with a strong, bright light.

Affirmation

"I have the courage and strength to be who I truly am."

RUTILATED QUARTZ

Physical Aspects

Rutilated quartz is clear quartz with needles of brown rutile or titanium dioxide scattered throughout. The mineral rutile is slightly less hard at 6–6½ than quartz and is of igneous and metamorphic origin. The rutile needles can vary in color due to the heat exposure they receive during the solidification process in quartz. Rutilated quartz can be found all over the world.

The Rutilated Quartz Deva

''With my deep and penetrating energy, I seek areas within your being where you need to 'get to the core of the matter' and release imbalanced thought patterns that have outlived their usefulness. I maintain a sustained intensity of focused light so that you can more clearly see the thoughts you need to release.

"You may have wondered if it is possible to program my species, and the answer is yes indeed. An ideal program would utilize the energy capacities of both quartz and rutile. You are encouraged to experiment with this in your own practice.

"Because I am a catalyst to bring greater clarity and understanding to your life experiences, I can reorder and balance an area after clearing has taken place. This is particularly true if the amounts of quartz and rutile are roughly equal in the stone.

"Greater conscious expansion is occurring on the spiritual levels of your being. The quality of life-force energies that you receive into your energy field is being continuously refined to support you in your chosen service on the Planet in this present lifetime."

Spiritual Aspects

Soul Tone: All tones
Chakra Affinities: All Chakras
Subtle Body Affinities: All Bodies
Energy Focus: Clearing
Element: Fire

Co-creating with Rutilated Quartz

Rutilated quartz will clear at the level or levels where the need is greatest, and that is where you will feel its action most strongly. As an essence, rutilated quartz can sometimes relieve minor pain such as headaches. Emotionally and mentally, rutilated quartz has an incisive quality that can be utilized to release troubled thoughts and feelings after a trying day, or before going to bed. It can be helpful when you are working on chronic habitual thought patterns. If you are feeling overly vulnerable as you begin working with rutilated quartz, you can focus on the clarity of quartz filling you with protective, expanding light. Rutilated quartz can give a sense of clarity and freedom, and it is very versatile as an emergency tension releaser.

Affirmation

"I can now see clearly beyond the illusions of my past."

SAPPHIRE

Physical Aspects

Sapphire, like ruby, belongs to the corundum family and occurs in blue, clear, pink, orange, yellow, green, purple, and black. Red corundum is called ruby, as we have stated earlier. Sapphire is an aluminum oxide with a hardness of 9, and it belongs to the trigonal system. Blue sapphire gets its coloring from iron and titanium. The other colors are due to varying amounts of these minerals as well as chrome and vanadium.

The main sapphire-bearing rocks are marble, basalt, and pegmatite. Mining is a simple, labor-intensive process. Gravel from hand-dug holes is panned with water and searched by hand. Most of the gem-quality sapphires come from the Orient in Burma, Thailand, India, and Sri Lanka. Light blue sapphires are found in Montana. Clear sapphire is a trade name for pure corundum. We will discuss the clear and light blue sapphires from Montana.

Clear Sapphire Deva

''My energies deepen your inner faith, so that in any circumstance you can reassure yourself that all is well. You express the quality of faith when you stand alone with commitment to your spiritual purpose. Faith is built internally and the quality of faith is also transmitted to you from the spirit world. Through me you can learn that the practice of optimistic faith and trust brings healing.

''It is also faith that inspires you to reach toward a greater expansion of Light. As you overcome your doubts and trust the process of your spiritual growth, you may sense your crown chakra opening. This open-ing is a vital first step to exploring other spiritual di-mensions.''

Clear Sapphire—Spiritual Aspects

Soul Tone: A#
Chakra Affinities: Crown (1), Third Eye (1)
Subtle Body Affinities: Emotional/Mental, Spiritual, Etheric
Energy Focus: Clearing, Building
Element: Fire/Air

Co-creating with Clear Sapphire

Clear sapphire can aid you in gently releasing unneeded, im-balanced energy so that you can continue to grow and heal. If, for example, you have a health problem for which medical an-swers are unsatisfactory, clear sapphire can open your aware-ness to the possibilities of spiritual healing. If you or a client are new to particular concepts of spiritual energy and higher spiri-tual awareness, clear sapphire inspires reassurance and a strong sense of the presence of Light and Love.

Clear Sapphire Affirmation

"I have faith and trust in the process of my growth toward the Light."

Blue Sapphire Deva

''When you seek to expand spiritually, you may need to be nurtured and supported in your practice of faith. I fill you with a compassionate, eternal peace that creates a calm environment for you to expand your spiritual sensitivities.''

Blue Sapphire—Spiritual Aspects

Soul Tone: A
Chakra Affinities: Third Eye (1)
Subtle Body Affinities: Emotional/Mental, Spiritual, Etheric
Energy Focus: Clearing, Building
Element: Fire/Air

Co-creating with Blue Sapphire

When there has been emotional pain and trauma, the inspiring and peaceful qualities of blue sapphire can move you from feeling encumbered to feeling free. Blue sapphire can strengthen your faith, so that you can release self-judgment and move into a healing space of Unconditional Love.

Blue Sapphire Affirmation

"Knowing that I am actively guided and supported in my growth toward the Light brings me peace."

SELENITE

Physical Aspects

Selenite is the clear variety of gypsum. It is a very soft hydrous calcium sulfate with a hardness of 1½–2 and a monoclinic crystalline structure. Selenite crystals are often rather flat and rhombic in shape. Gypsum is a common sulphate mineral that develops principally in sedimentary rocks. Good crystals are found in Mexico and the U.S. Selenite is not considered a gemstone because it is too soft and sensitive to cut for jewelry, but like other minerals, it has a place in healing. We work with the clear and cloudy white selenite.

The Selenite Deva

"My energies can help you access the Spirit Guides that support you on your life path, for I wish to reassure you that you are not alone in this life. If you wish to know your Spirit Guides, work with me in a meditative, receptive state and visualize yourself surrounded by Pure White Light. Affirm in your thoughts the desire to know the essence of the Spirit Guides that are near you. I encourage you to ask, 'What is your purpose for being in a dialogue with me?' Your Guides come not to change you, but to support you in your growth.

"Your Guides are Spirit Beings who have been on the Earth Plane and choose to continue their service in the area in which they worked while on the Earth. This is not usually done until additional knowledge and awareness has been assimilated. They match their expertise to a lifestream such as yourself that is following a similar path on the Earth. First, the Spirit Being mentally approaches the lifestream and observes the energy pattern. If the energy pattern becomes discordant, then the Spirit Being discontinues contact for a period of time. If further contact is desired by the lifestream, then the Spirit Guide initiates that contact through the crown center of the lifestream. Once the foundation has been set for communication, the process can be refined and expanded. I say, open yourself to the World of Spirit to help you understand and work through your Earth Plane experiences."

Spiritual Aspects

Soul Tone: A#, A, depending on the individual stone.
Chakra Affinities: Crown (1), Third Eye (1)
Subtle Body Affinities: Spiritual
Energy Focus: Spiritual Expansion
Element: Air

Co-creating with Selenite

Selenite is a gentle crown and third eye-opener. Work with the stone when you wish to contact your Spirit Guides. Individual selenite stones seem to vary more in their individual frequencies than some others. Chakra affinity and compatibility with other stones needs to be checked with each individual selenite.

Affirmation

"I affirm my connection with my Spirit Guides."

SMOKY QUARTZ

Physical Aspects

Smoky quartz is a pale brown to black silicon dioxide with a hardness of 7 and a trigonal crystalline structure. It is frequently found with inclusions of rutile. Sometimes it is heat-treated to make the color lighter. Smoky quartz is found in Brazil, Switzerland, Colorado, and New Hampshire.

Smoky Quartz Deva

''I give you a sense of emotional security that allows you to be open to new experiences. I reassure you that you will not fail in your new endeavors. I remind you that it is not important whether you win or lose. What is important is that you learn and let your experiences give you understanding that will be helpful to you later.''

Spiritual Aspects

Soul Tone: C
Chakra Affinities: Root (1), Lower Abdomen (2), Solar Plexus (2)
Subtle Body Affinities: Emotional/Mental, Etheric, Spiritual
Energy Focus: Building
Element: Water

Co-creating with Smoky Quartz

Smoky quartz stabilizes the emotions and can reassure you on an ongoing basis whenever you fear failure. It also encourages you to experience new things and develop an attitude of self-acceptance in the learning process.

Affirmation

"I find security in knowing that I can learn, whether I win or lose."

SODALITE

Physical Aspects

Sodalite is similar in appearance to lapis lazuli, except that it is often a deeper, more striking indigo blue. It is a sodium aluminum silicate with chlorine and has a hardness of 5½–6 and an isometric crystalline structure. The larger deposits are in Canada and Brazil, and it is also found in the U.S.

The Sodalite Deva

"I help to bring order and calmness, primarily at your mental level, but extending to what you verbally express. Focus goes hand in hand with order, and mental focus is achieved when you can slow and still your mind of incessant chatter. When your mind is ordered, then there is no wasted energy through the impulsive expression of irrelevant thoughts. I help you to think clearly and say what you mean. When your conscious mind is still you will know whether the guidance you are receiving is coming from your Higher Guidance or from some other part of you. Effortless choices are made in a state of calm, ordered peace."

Spiritual Aspects

Soul Tone: A, A#
Chakra Affinities: Third Eye (1)
Subtle Body Affinities: Mental, Spiritual, Etheric
Energy Focus: Building
Element: Air/Earth

Co-creating with Sodalite

When a fan is running, the blades look like an undifferentiated mass, but when the motor is slowed down or turned off, the noise level drops and you can see the individual blades. Sodalite is like the fan motor. It aids the conscious mind through slowing down and stilling it, so that you can identify and clarify the key mental points. Therefore it is helpful if you have a tendency to mental panic when fearful, or if you are indecisive at times.

It can be helpful to take sodalite essence before you begin to meditate, or to hold the stone during meditation. Sodalite calms and stills the chattering conscious mind so that you can achieve a single-pointed focus more easily. Sodalite aids concentration and mental discipline, so that your mind doesn't wander off the subject.

Affirmation

"My mind is calm and ordered, so that I can concentrate with a singular focus."

SPINEL (RED)

Physical Aspects

Although spinel comes in red, blue, violet, and brown, it is the red spinel that is most often seen in the gem trade. Red spinel has often been confused with ruby, because they are similar in hardness and brilliance. Spinel is a magnesium aluminum oxide with a hardness of 8 and an isometric crystalline structure. Like ruby it gets its red color from traces of chromium. Spinel crystallizes in an octahedral shape and forms in plutonic and metamorphic rocks. Spinel is easily manufactured: yellow, green, and clear spinels are usually synthetic. Blue spinel is widely used as a substitute for aquamarine. Spinel is found chiefly in the gem gravels of Sri Lanka, Burma, and Thailand. It is also found in Brazil and the U.S. We have worked with the red spinel.

The Red Spinel Deva

''I can help you reconnect with the power that is you. When you seek recognition and approval from others, then you create meaning for your life which is dependent on the beliefs and love of others. If you deny aspects of your being that are truly a unique part of your self-expression, you may lack enjoyment in life, or not feel connected to your creative tasks. I help you recognize and affirm your Inner Self, so that you can truly live, instead of merely existing according to patterns set by others. When you feel that your life may be meaningless, I can connect you with feelings you have hidden, or gifts you have not expressed. If your life has meaning, and you have inner recognition of Self, then you will have the inner drive in all circumstances to complete what you start. Completion of your tasks is its own fulfillment, and your sense of who you are is strengthened.''

Spiritual Aspects

Soul Tone: E
Chakra Affinities: Solar Plexus (1)
Subtle Body Affinities: Emotional/Mental
Energy Focus: Clearing
Element: Fire

Co-creating with Red Spinel

Red spinel affirms your resourcefulness when you are holding back from committing yourself to a project or service. It diminishes timidity and reluctance and increases willingness and confidence when you are dealing with beliefs about not being good enough. It helps dissolve self-judgment and criticism and affirms inner recognition. Red spinel, with its fiery energy, inspires you to finish projects you have started.

Affirmation

"I am resourceful and capable of finishing what I start."

SUGILITE

Physical Aspects

Sugilite is a uniquely colored reddish-violet stone that has been described as looking like grape jelly. It is a potassium ferric lithium silicate with a hardness of 6–6½ and a hexagonal crystalline structure. The trace mineral manganese gives the pink-lavender color. Although it was discovered in Japan in 1944, cuttable sugilite was not known until 1975, when a gem-quality deposit was found in South Africa. Other deposits are located in India. You may also find sugilite referred to as royal luvulite, royal azel, and cybeline.

The Sugilite Deva

''Whenever you make reference to what separates you from others through imbalanced thoughts and feelings, my energies reaffirm your true Divine Nature as Unconditional Love. If you are suffering from physical imbalance, I say to you that at this time you are choosing the physical vehicle as the optimal way in which to learn about self-acceptance and Unconditional Love. Whenever you are feeling judgmental toward yourself, my energies can help you to see the Light within you that is eternally connected to the Divine Source. Accept and value yourself as you truly are, and an enduring healing on all levels will take place.''

Spiritual Aspects

Soul Tone: A#
Chakra Affinities: Third Eye (1), Crown (2)
Subtle Body Affinities: Spiritual, Emotional/Mental
Energy Focus: Building, Clearing
Element: Water

Co-creating with Sugilite

Sugilite teaches a lesson that is sometimes very hard to grasp at the gut level: we are truly manifestations of Unconditional Love. Sugilite is very flowing and self-affirming, and through its energies we can understand that we are like angels in physical form; we are precious Divine Beings. When you are working with a physical imbalance, meditate with sugilite to help you dialogue with the specific body part in question and to understand what you need to affirm. Then you can visualize yourself as already whole and perfectly healthy. Sugilite can also aid in dissolving overly judgmental attitudes toward yourself and others that may keep you feeling separate.

Affirmation

"I am a Divine Manifestation of Love."

SUNSTONE (ORANGE)

Physical Aspects

Orange sunstone is a sodium calcium aluminum silicate member of the feldspar family and is also called aventurine feldspar or oligoclase. Its coloring is orange-brown with a metallic glitter. Orange sunstone has a hardness of 6–6½ and a triclinic crystalline structure. Sunstone can be found in the U.S., India, Canada, South Norway, and Russia. *For information on yellow sunstone, see yellow orthoclase feldspar.*

Orange Sunstone Deva

''I help you to grow from any fears that you may have related to the expansion of Self. When you can repeatedly see yourself as a vibrant, vital, confident being, this pattern becomes impressed as a thought form into the subconscious mind. I work with your physical body, giving you a sense of expansion and vitality at that level. As a catalyst in your expansion on the emotional and mental levels, I tell you that you are now greater than you have ever been, and send you impressions of this way of perceiving yourself. You determine the degree of expansion that you are willing to accept. In truth you are a limitless being, with many opportunities to bring greater Light to your physical body and your physical world.''

Spiritual Aspects

Soul Tone: D#
Chakra Affinities: Root (1), Lower Abdomen (1)
Subtle Body Affinities: Etheric, Emotional/Mental, Spiritual
Energy Focus: Building
Element: Water

Co-creating with Orange Sunstone

Orange sunstone has a sunny vitality and an expansiveness that can get you moving again if you have limited your possibilities in life. It gently and lovingly encourages you not to take life's setbacks to heart and to *think big*. Explore and expand your possibilities and know that the sky is the limit.

Affirmation

"There is no limit to what I can do."

TIGER'S EYE

Physical Aspects

Tiger's eye is a brown quartz silicon dioxide with lustrous yellow and brown parallel fibers. It has a hardness of 7 and belongs to the trigonal system. The yellow-gold colors are due to iron oxides. Tiger's eye has the property of chatoyancy, which means that it glimmers with a small ray of light on the surface, like the eyes of a cat. The largest deposits of tiger's eye are in South Africa, Australia, Burma, India, and the U.S.

The Tiger's Eye Deva

"Your personal will and the emotions that accompany it are intricately related to the proper use of power. When your will is in harmony with your Higher Will, your self-confidence is maximally enhanced. I help you act wisely in your everyday life and I keep your feet firmly planted on the ground. True power is built patiently from small steps. Each step is an act of will that is in harmony with your intuitive sense of rightness and accomplished with perseverance."

Spiritual Aspects

Soul Tone: C#
Chakra Affinities: Root (1), Solar Plexus (1), Lower Abdomen (1)
Subtle Body Affinities: Etheric, Emotional/Mental
Energy Focus: Building
Element: Earth/Fire

Co-creating with Tiger's Eye

When you feel as though your daily activities are not getting you anywhere, tiger's eye teaches you to affirm a purpose to your activities. Perhaps you are building endurance and patience. The foundation of a house lies mostly underground and must be carefully laid out and very well built. Affirm that your activities are building a foundation of self-reliance, which then becomes your personal power.

Affirmation

"My personal power comes from my belief in my purpose and my strength."

TOPAZ

Physical Aspects

The most popular color of topaz is yellow, and in antiquity all yellow stones were called topaz. The term "precious topaz" is used today to refer to an aluminum flurosilicate that comes in clear, blue, yellow, and pink colors. It is formed under the influence of fluorine and water during the formation of granite pegmatites. Topaz has a hardness of 8 and an orthorhombic crystalline structure. It has a perfect cleavage, so care must be taken in cutting. Russia is a source for gem-quality blue topaz, and Brazil is well known for its clear and yellow topaz. Other deposits are located in Sri Lanka, Burma, and the U.S. Sometimes citrine and heat-treated amethysts are sold as "gold topaz" or "Madeira topaz." True topaz is often called "precious topaz," as we stated earlier. Yellow topaz is also often referred to as "imperial topaz." Sometimes the clear variety is irradiated to make a sky blue color.

We will first discuss clear topaz, and then move to yellow and blue topaz.

The Clear Topaz Deva

"My purpose is to inspire the expansion of your mental and intuitive faculties. I broaden your comprehension of spiritual truth. You must decide whether a particular understanding can be connected with other beliefs so that a continuity is established. If not, then I say 'travel light.' Do not weigh down your existence with a disordered mind. As I expand the channel of Light that connects you with your Higher Self, seek the Oneness, Joy, and Beauty that is part of all Spiritual Truth."

Clear Topaz—Spiritual Aspects

Soul Tone: A#
Chakra Affinities: Third Eye (1), Crown (2)
Subtle Body Affinities: Spiritual, Mental, Etheric
Energy Focus: Building
Element: Air

Co-creating with Clear Topaz

Clear topaz aids in the birth of new understanding. With its joyful, active, uplifting energies it can help you change knowledge to wisdom. Working with topaz is like reading a book about personal growth or spiritual wisdom and having an "aha" experience. You suddenly "get" what the author is trying to say. Utilize clear topaz whenever you are reading or studying, in order to assimilate new spiritual wisdom. Topaz keeps you from being discouraged when you don't understand something. Also, when you wish to better understand what you are to learn from a recent experience, try working with clear topaz.

Clear Topaz Affirmation

"I joyfully expand the horizons of my spiritual understanding."

The Yellow Topaz Deva

''Like clear topaz, my energies can help to expand the higher creative capacities of your mind. As your conscious awareness becomes more elevated, you see life from a broader viewpoint. That viewpoint then needs to be implemented in your physical world. My energies contain two specific qualities that foster this process within you. First, I can give an inherent recognition that this new understanding has practical application. Second, my energies instill a desire to integrate this seed essence into a manifestation.''

Yellow Topaz—Spiritual Aspects

Soul Tone: E
Chakra Affinities: Solar Plexus (1), Third Eye (1)
Subtle Body Affinities: Mental, Spiritual, Etheric
Energy Focus: Building
Element: Air

Co-creating with Yellow Topaz

Yellow topaz helps you to simplify the wisdom and understanding you receive, so that you can assimilate it in your conscious mind in a way that is conducive to practical application. Yellow topaz can stimulate innovative ideas for any project or research. Yellow topaz together with citrine is a wonderful combination for the student or researcher.

Yellow Topaz Affirmation

"I seek to comprehend the practical wisdom in all my experience, and I manifest that wisdom."

The Blue Topaz Deva

''Many times when a lifestream has experienced expansion on the mental and spiritual levels, frustration and doubt surface, as comparisons are made with the present beliefs and attitudes about self. My energies bring you a sense of peace and reassurance. No one is saying that the experiences gained through mental and spiritual expansion are going to blend in perfectly with how you view life. Give yourself the permission and space to assimilate new understandings into your consciousness in a gentle, loving way. Remember that questioning the meaning of things is natural and acceptable. I tell you that the pure essence of your knowing is what will find its right space in your reality, however you perceive it to be.''

Blue Topaz—Spiritual Aspects

Soul Tone: A
Chakra Affinities: Third Eye (1)
Subtle Body Affinities: Emotional/Mental, Spiritual, Etheric
Energy Focus: Building
Element: Air

Co-creating with Blue Topaz

Blue topaz works similarly to clear topaz, but its energies are calmer and more peaceful. Blue topaz can help you accept new ideas when you feel agitated by the discrepancies created in your belief systems. Blue topaz does not seem to combine as well with other stones as clear topaz.

Blue Topaz Affirmation

"I calmly accept the implications of my expanding spiritual understanding."

TOURMALINE

Physical Aspects

Like the quartz family, tourmalines come in a wide variety of colors and have been popular semi-precious gemstones. Tourmaline is a complex borosilicate with a hardness of 7 and a trigonal crystalline structure. In their rough form, tourmaline crystals are typically prismatic and heavily striated. When they are cut and polished they can be easily confused with other stones of similar colors. You can see different color tints, depending on which direction the light is traveling through the crystal. This means that if a dark crystal is cut with its flat part or table parallel to the long axis, the color will be lightened. Conversely, a lighter tourmaline cut perpendicular to the long axis will appear deeper in color. Like quartz, tourmaline also has piezoelectric properties. By heating or cooling it, or applying a mechanical pressure, you can electrically charge a tourmaline so that one end becomes negative and the other becomes positive.

Tourmaline is a common stone in granite pegmatites, so their occurance is widespread. In the U.S., gem-quality tourmaline comes from Maine and California. Elsewhere, tourmaline is mined in the Urals in Russia, Sri Lanka, the Malagasy Republic, and Brazil.

The different colors of tourmaline have some varying properties. Therefore, the most common varieties for healing will be discussed separately. They include green, pink, watermelon, black, and blue tourmaline. *Black tourmalinated quartz is included under black tourmaline.*

Green Tourmaline—Physical Aspects

Green tourmaline, or elbaite, is the most common member of the tourmaline family. It gets its color from lithium, sodium, and potassium trace minerals. In fact, elbaite is sometimes called lithium tourmaline. The most valued color is an emerald green, and sometimes the darker green tourmaline is heated to approximately one thousand degrees fahrenheit to produce this green.

The Green Tourmaline Deva

"Through my energies you can learn to be committed to your goals and at the same time be non-attached to the process and its outcome. Non-attachment means that you allow yourself to step aside from the creative form of your goal and allow it to grow and expand from the original focus. When there are disruptions in the flow you make adjustments to restimulate the flow, so that your decisions come from the perspective of an overall direction. The steps you take to restimulate the flow also energize the thought form of the original goal. However, I also tell you that you do not need to worry about each little step along the way. You can trust that the flow is like a river, taking you where you want to go, even when you go through little backwater whirlpools or meandering sidestreams. You will find balance in letting go of your attachments to how your life needs to be."

Green Tourmaline—Spiritual Aspects

Soul Tone: E
Chakra Affinities: Solar Plexus (1), Lower Abdomen (1)
Subtle Body Affinities: Emotional/Mental, Etheric, Spiritual
Energy Focus: Building
Element: Water

Co-creating with Green Tourmaline

Green tourmaline gives emotional balance through helping you let go of expectations about how things should be. It helps you detach from a situation in a nonjudgmental way. Green tourmaline can calm anxiety as you go for job interviews or when your life takes an unexpected turn. If you find yourself worrying or saying "what if," as you prepare for an endeavor, green tourmaline will calm you. Green tourmaline has a way of balancing emotional highs and lows so that you can let whatever happens happen with more equanimity.

"Ask for what you want, but don't demand it.
Accept whatever happens for now.
Turn up your light even if you don't get what you want."
—Ken Keyes

Green Tourmaline Affirmation

"I let go of my inner attachments about how my life needs to be."

Pink Tourmaline—Physical Aspects

Pink tourmaline, or rubellite, ranges in color from pink to red. A ruby red is the most valued color of tourmaline in the gem trade. Red and pink tourmaline get their color from a combination of trace elements, including lithium, sodium, and potassium.

The Pink Tourmaline Deva

''I teach you that Unconditional Love cannot be possessed or manipulated. My energies help you to clear your attachment about how love 'should' be expressed in an experience. When your expectations become too high or too fixed, and the object of your devotion deviates from those expectations, I challenge you to let go of your expectations. I can also help you remain in a state of balance by teaching you to enjoy the flow of your life, wherever it takes you.''

Pink Tourmaline—Spiritual Aspects

Soul Tone: D
Chakra Affinities: Lower Abdomen (1), Heart (1), Solar Plexus (2)
Subtle Body Affinities: Emotional/Mental, Etheric, Spiritual
Energy Focus: Building
Element: Water

Co-creating with Pink Tourmaline

Pink tourmaline is also helpful for a nonattached acceptance of things, and it has a more energetic, uplifting quality to it. You can work with it in a relationship when you wish to cut back on demanding that the other needs to change in order for you to be happy.

Pink Tourmaline Affirmation

"I accept you without judgment and without expectations."

Watermelon Tourmaline—Physical Aspects

Watermelon tourmaline is a descriptive name given to a tourmaline that is red or pink inside and green outside. Polished cross sections are particularly striking.

The Watermelon Tourmaline Deva:

''From the moment that a lifestream incarnates into a physical vehicle, it comes into contact with other lifestreams who seek to pattern the new lifestream's energy according to their own beliefs and desires. I help you to learn the art of detachment through discernment, to identify who you are and who you are not in relationship to others. As you seek to change your point of reference in how you view yourself, my energy, through the power of Unconditional Love, helps you to release false identifications which do not reflect your true Self. My synergistic blend of energies can unlock the door to greater self-acceptance and greater expansion on your spiritual path.''

Watermelon Tourmaline—Spiritual Aspects

Soul Tone: D# when the piece has more pink, E when it has more green.
Chakra Affinities: Lower Abdomen (1), Heart (1), Solar Plexus (2)
Subtle Body Affinities: Emotional/Mental, Etheric, Spiritual
Energy Focus: Building
Element: Water

Co-creating with Watermelon Tourmaline

Watermelon tourmaline blends the calm equanimity of green tourmaline with the more energetic upliftment of pink tourmaline. You could utilize it in situations where either pink or green tourmaline is appropriate.

Watermelon Tourmaline Affirmation

"I calmly release the expectations of others."

Black Tourmaline and Black Tourmalinated Quartz—Physical Aspects

Black tourmaline is also called schorl. The black color is due in part to traces of iron. Although black tourmaline is very common, its energies seem to us quite "heavy," so we prefer to utilize black tourmalinated quartz, which is clear quartz with inclusions of black tourmaline.

The Black Tourmalinated Quartz Deva

''My energies can give you a sense of protection and safety. Minerals do not just happen to bond their energy vibrations together by sheer chance. I can teach the Human Kingdom that light and darkness are not in mutual opposition. The clear quartz that is a part of my structure can amplify your sense of being surrounded and protected by the Light. The black tourmaline in my structure gives you a sense of safety. Each mineral works independently and yet we both work as one. The beauty and flexibility of my vibrations are such that you can program me to resonate to a particular color in your energy field to enhance the energy already present there.''

Black Tourmalinated Quartz—Spiritual Aspects

Soul Tone: Black Tourmaline—C. Black Tourmalinated Quartz —all tones.
Chakra Affinities: Black Tourmaline—Root (1). Black Tourmalinated Quartz—all chakras.
Subtle Body Affinities: Emotional/Mental, Etheric, Spiritual
Energy Focus: Building
Element: Earth

Co-creating with Black Tourmalinated Quartz

The lightness and clarity of clear quartz amplifies the combination of emotional protection and balance of the black tourmaline. This energy is helpful for relationships in which you need to let go of expectations and need a sense of emotional protection and safety as well. Black tourmaline gives a quality of inner security, like being in a womb.

Black Tourmalinated Quartz Affirmation

"I am emotionally safe and protected."

Blue Tourmaline—Physical Aspects

Blue tourmaline is also called indicolite. Its dark blue color is due to traces of iron.

Blue Tourmaline Deva

''Like the other tourmalines, I teach you that both worrying about how things are happening, and desiring things to happen in a certain way only slow down your expansion. In addition, I say to you to value truth as you understand it, no matter what others are doing. In doing so you may operate with or against the expectations of others. Remember that your purpose is to be in rhythm with the Greater Harmonies of the Universe and to trust that by doing this you will have fulfilled your spiritual service. In this way you flow with focus.''

Blue Tourmaline—Spiritual Aspects

Soul Tone: E
Chakra Affinities: Solar Plexus (1), Third Eye (1), Throat (2)
Subtle Body Affinities: Emotional/Mental, Spiritual, Etheric
Energy Focus: Building
Element: Water

Co-creating with Blue Tourmaline

Whenever you feel conflict between your Inner Spiritual Voice and the expectations of others, blue tourmaline can strengthen your understanding of the appropriate course of action. In this way you learn to value your own intuition and not to be swayed by the norms and values of society.

Blue Tourmaline Affirmation

"Following the beat of my own drummer, I do what is right for me on my spiritual path, and I release the expectations of others."

TURQUOISE

Physical Aspects

Turquoise, sometimes called callais, is an opaque stone that ranges from sky blue and blue-green to apple-green. It is a hydrous phosphate of aluminum and copper, with a hardness of 5–6 and a triclinic crystalline structure. The pure blue color is rare, and traces of iron make it more green in color.

Turquoise is most commonly found in a matrix with veins of dark brown limonite, dark gray sandstone, black jasper, green malachite, and blue-green chrysocolla. The best quality occurs in nodules rather than veins, in northeastern Iran and Afghanistan. Turquoise is also mined the southwestern U.S., Australia, and China.

Turquoise is very porous and is often impregnated with wax or plastic to deepen the color and add durability. There are several ways to tell whether turquoise has been impregnated. When turquoise has been plastic-bonded, you can carefully scrape it with a penknife and it will peel rather than powder, and give off an odor when heated. If it has been heavily waxed, a heated needle applied to the surface will melt the wax. Sometimes it is also dyed to deepen the color.

The Turquoise Deva

"I teach you that Planet Earth and everything on it is a living, Spiritual Consciousness. I operate within your Spiritual Awareness rather than your conscious knowing. My energies help you to attune your vibrational energies to the Spiritual Essence within Nature's Mineral, Plant and Animal Kingdoms.

I teach you about giving as well as receiving, not only from Planet Earth but from your own Kingdom as well. If you of the Human Kingdom continue to hold the belief that you can 'take' from Planet Earth and her Kingdoms without giving in return, you will not fully understand how the quality of your life has been reduced. I am a catalyst for initiating changes concerning your true relationship to the Earth. In this way you will heal the Earth Mother as well as yourselves."

Spiritual Aspects

Soul Tone: F#
Chakra Affinities: Heart (1), Thymus Gland (1)
Subtle Body Affinities: Spiritual, Etheric
Energy Focus: Spiritual Expansion
Element: Air/Earth

Co-creating with Turquoise

Turquoise strengthens the desire to be Earth stewards, and can be helpful when you wish to connect with the Mineral,

Plant, or Animal Kingdoms. Turquoise strengthens your awareness of the interconnectedness of all life and is useful if you are feeling separate from others or from the natural world around you. Turquoise can also teach you to honor your physical body. Its gentle sense of interconnectedness has a healing effect and strengthens your awareness that we are all healers.

Affirmation

"I am One with the Earth, and I honor all life with love and respect."

YELLOW ORTHOCLASE FELDSPAR (YELLOW SUNSTONE)

Physical Aspects

Yellow orthoclase feldspar is a cloudy, yellow-green stone that is sometimes called yellow sunstone. However, it has a different chemical composition from orange sunstone, so we have taken the liberty of giving it a name that is descriptive of its mineral family. It is a potassium aluminum silicate member of the feldspar family with a hardness of 6–6½. Gem-quality orthoclase is found in the Malagasy Republic and Upper Burma. There are also plentiful deposits in the U.S.

The Yellow Orthoclase Feldspar Deva

''I help fine-tune your sense of timing in the activities of your life. Sometimes you choose to do things on emotional impulse, which can be unnecessarily risky. On other occasions you oversaturate yourself with information before you move on a decision. You may give more of your life-force energy to this process than you need to. I can help you find the middle road by heightening your perception of when it is time to make your decision and act on it. I give you a sense of reassurance that your decision is in a harmonious flow with the long-term goals you have for yourself. I can keep you from worrying about the 'what ifs' so that you have a sense of flowing and being free for the expansion taking place in your life."

Spiritual Aspects

Soul Tone: *E, D#* Lighter stones test E. Darker and more
    opaque stones test D#.
Chakra Affinities: Solar Plexus (1), Lower Abdomen (2)
Subtle Body Affinities: Emotional/Mental, Etheric, Spiritual
Energy Focus: Building
Element: Water

Co-creating with Yellow Orthoclase Feldspar

If you are strongly attracted to yellow orthoclase feldspar at a particular time, you are probably being given a message that it is now time to make a move that you have been contemplating in some area of your life. It helps to keep you flowing so that you do not get bogged down in minor concerns and lose your focus. Yellow orthoclase feldspar thus helps with vacillation, indecision, and hesitancy through its warm, steady optimism and confidence.

Affirmation

"I move forward confidently on my path."

THE METALS

Gold, silver, and copper are metallic elements which are included in this section to show how their energies combine in jewelry and other healing applications. Because the quality of their energy is more generalized or broadly focused than that of the minerals, they are more versatile in their use.

COPPER

Physical Aspects

Copper is a metallic element (Cu) that can exist in a free, uncombined state. Besides the color of new pennies, copper can be black, blue, or green. It is a heavy, malleable mineral with a hardness of 2½–3 and an isometric crystalline structure. Copper is mined in Michigan, Arizona, New Mexico, and Nova Scotia.

The Copper Deva

"I seek to restimulate the flow of life-force energies where there has been constriction. My domain is the etheric subtle body and the physical vehicle itself. In order for me to be effective in your physical vehicle, you must be willing to change, for it is a restrictive way of thinking that causes an immobilization of life-force energy. Once the flow of life-force energy has been restored, other minerals such as clear quartz crystal can expand that flow. I can truly open your being so that you can relate to your Spiritual Nature in a more dynamic way."

Spiritual Aspects

Soul Tone: D
Chakra Affinities: Thymus Gland (1)
Subtle Body Affinities: Etheric, Spiritual
Energy Focus: Clearing
Element: Fire

Co-creating with Copper

Copper combines well in jewelry with stones that work in a clearing, dispersing capacity. It naturally occurs with malachite, azurite, and chrysocolla, and enhances their effect on the physical body. You can combine clear quartz crystal and copper by partially wrapping a crystal with copper wire, or making a wand with copper tubing and clear quartz crystal at the end. The copper will clear dense, imbalanced energy at the etheric subtle level, creating "space" for the amplification of life-force energies by the crystal. This combination gives a sense of movement and increased energy flow which is very effective for healing. A copper pyramid works in a similar manner.

Affirmation

"Life-force energy is now flowing smoothly throughout my body, giving me greater health and vitality."

GOLD

Physical Aspects

Gold is a metallic element (Au) that occurs in a free, uncombined state and rarely combines with other elements. It has a hardness of 2½–3 and an isometric crystalline structure. Gold is heavier than pyrite and can yield a powder when hit with a hammer. It is currently mined in California, Colorado, Mexico, and Ontario.

The Gold Deva

"My purpose is to enhance your connection with your Divine Nature so that you can reflect who you truly are. You can convert my energies to those qualities that enhance your self-identity and thereby affect your physical well-being. The quality of my energy is like the Sun, and it has an activating effect on your energy system. The Sun is a primary source of life-force energies. Like other stones, I radiate stored life-force energies that are originally from the Sun throughout your being."

Spiritual Aspects

Soul Tone: E
Chakra Affinities: Root (1), Solar Plexus (1), Throat (1), Crown
    (1), Thymus Gland (1)
Subtle Body Affinities: Spiritual, Etheric
Energy Focus: Building
Element: Fire

Co-creating with Gold

Gold can amplify the life-force energy of stones with which it is combined. The amplification is strongest with stones that have a chakra affinity that is similar to the chakra affinities of gold. You can wear stones at the thymus gland with a gold chain and affirm your connection with your Divine Nature.

Affirmation

"I am actualizing my highest potential."

SILVER

Physical Aspects

Silver is a metallic element (Ag) that can be found in an un-combined state, although deposits sometimes include gold, mercury, copper, and other minerals. Besides its silvery color, it comes in whitish gray, yellow, brown, and black. Silver has a hardness of 2½–3 and an isometric crystalline structure. It is widely distributed in small amounts, but the largest mines are in Michigan, Arizona, Colorado, Ontario, and Mexico.

The Silver Deva

"I function primarily in the emotional subtle body as a gentle mover of energies that have become restricted or immobilized. My broadly focused energy can return you to emotional and mental stability. Since I am a single mineral I have more versatility in my function than a composite of minerals, which takes on a more specialized role. Work with me wherever you seek to grow, and I will help you begin the process of change."

Spiritual Aspects

Soul Tone: D
Chakra Affinities: Root (1), Lower Abdomen (1), Heart (1) Third
    Eye (1), Crown (2)
Subtle Body Affinities: Emotional, Spiritual

Energy Focus: Clearing
Element: Water

Co-creating with Silver

Silver settings can amplify stones with a similar chakra affinity. Silver jewelry can be worn at the heart to help you release constriction which keeps you from receiving and giving Unconditional Love. In general, silver can increase your sensitivity to your emotional nature. Its energies are gentle, harmonizing, and flowing.

Affirmation

"I am in harmony with my emotional body."

PART THREE

Co-Creating with Gemstones for Healing

Now that you have been introduced to the individual stones, we can discuss ways to work with gemstones for healing yourself and others. Chapter 6 describes how to make and utilize gem essences for internal use. The use of essences has become more widespread since Edward Bach developed his flower remedies in the 1930s. In Chapter 7 we discuss some ways in which you can utilize one or two stones on the body for healing. Chapters 8, 9, and 10 are devoted to finely attuned combinations of stones that serve a specific purpose. These combinations have been developed with particular attention to how the energy qualities blend together. We have integrated the crystal grid layouts from *The Newcastle Guide to Healing with Crystals* with a gemstone layout at the end of Chapters 8, 9, and 10, to give you examples of how they might be combined. Clear quartz crystal helps to amplify and integrate the more specific gemstone energies into the total energy field. Chapters 8 and 9 also conclude with summary charts on the gemstone chakra and soul-tone affinities and the layouts. Chapter 10 gives different ways of meditating with stones as well as the

157

spiritual expansion layouts. The book concludes with comments from the Devas on personal and Planetary Healing in Chapter 11. It doesn't really matter what particular methods we use for our healing process because we all work according to our own understanding. What does matter, however, is that the more we heal ourselves and others, the more we upgrade the quality of life for all on this Planet.

6 | Gem Essences: Their Use and Preparation

W<small>HEN YOU ARE</small> consciously working with attitudinal changes, gem essences can provide a balanced pattern of specific energy which operates like a subliminal tape, repeating positive messages over and over. However, also like a subliminal tape, it is sometimes hard to attribute changes directly to the essences. We have had experiences in which we noticed a dramatic release of discomfort in a given situation and other experiences in which it didn't seem like much happened. We are now able to sense the energy of the essences in our bodies, and have come to know more about how they work. Before that time we assumed on faith that they did work. You do not have to be aware of the essence in order for it to be effective. You just need to be willing to change.

This chapter includes some specific suggestions on making gem water and gem essences, and also how to go about choosing gem essences for yourself and others. At the end of the chapter there are charts that you can use with a pendulum in order to determine the essences needed. (Chapter 4 in *The Newcastle Guide to Healing With Crystals* gives a more complete discussion of how to work with a pendulum.) For easy reference, we

159

have also included a summary of the gemstone affirmations and soul tones at the end of the chapter.

Taking gem water internally is something like taking herbs for healing purposes. However, taking herbs can more directly affect the etheric subtle body and the physical body. We are focusing more on affecting the emotional, mental, and spiritual subtle bodies with minerals, with the assumption that ultimately our overall health will be improved.

MAKING GEM WATER AND GEM ESSENCES

After you have cleaned and charged your gemstones, it is good to use them to make structured water. We will refer to the structured water that you drink on a daily basis *gem water*. If you preserve the water and use it in eyedropper amounts, then we call it a *gem essence*. Gem essences have also been called gem remedies, gem elixirs, or gem tinctures.

Taking structured water internally is an excellent way to learn about the gemstones and to find out how the stones will work with your individual energies. The properties of the stones will give you some ideas about how the essences might work for you. It helps to keep records of how you are feeling when you take an essence, and the changes that occur. Then you will better know which stone you need in a given situation. You can develop your own rituals and methods for making gem waters and essences. Here are the steps we follow:

1. Place the stone in a clear glass container that has been sterilized by pouring boiling water into it. You can also place the glass container in an oven at 350 degrees for half an hour. If you are making gem water, you might want to use a gallon container such as the glass jars that restaurants sometimes use for mayonnaise and pickles. If you are making an essence, you can use smaller glass jars or containers.

2. Add spring or distilled water. In our experience, spring water is better. You can purchase either at the grocery store.

3. Cover the container and place it outside in the sun. (We have also tried this process indoors under a pyramid and it

does not work as well. Intuitively, we perceive that the Devas prefer to work outside of a pyramid.)

4.   Fill yourself with love and gratitude for the Elements of Nature and ask for Devic help in charging the water for healing.

5.   Leave the containers either for several hours, a day, or a day and a night, depending on the amount of water and your individual preferences. Gem water left out for twenty-four hours under the full moon carries the dynamic energies of both the sun and the moon. Moon energies are very beneficial for emotional healing.

Gem water used for drinking will last about three days at the most. If you wish to work with it on an ongoing basis, then you need to preserve it and it becomes a *gem essence*.

1.   You can buy one-ounce brown eyedropper bottles at the drugstore either singly, or in boxes of one or two dozen.

2.   Sterilize them in boiling water for fifteen minutes. Do not buy bottles with plastic eyedroppers because they bend when sterilized, and leave a taste in the essence. Also, they are not easy to resterilize.

3.   Fill the bottle halfway with your gem water.

4.   Fill the bottle the rest of the way with a good quality drinking alcohol such as brandy. (The alcohol is the only expensive part of this operation.) Now you have a gem essence that is fifty percent water and fifty percent alcohol.

5.   Label your bottles as "stock," such as "ruby stock," and store them under a pyramid or on a shelf out of the sunlight.

TAKING THE GEM ESSENCES

We will now describe two ways of taking the essences. The first is to put two to five drops from the stock bottle into a glass of spring water and sip it at intervals throughout the day. The second is to make up a bottle of the essence that you carry with you during the day.

1. Sterilize another brown one-ounce bottle and fill it one-third full with drinking alcohol.

2. Fill it the rest of the way with spring water. Add two or three drops of your stock and shake.

3. Label it, for example, "ruby essence," to distinguish it from other essences in your stock.

4. Take the drops under your tongue. You can also put the drops into a glass of water as you did with the stock. This practice will preserve your stock.

5. If you wish to reuse your bottles, be sure to sterilize them, especially the eyedroppers. Make sure that they are filled with boiling water and emptied. Boiling the bottles and droppers for twenty minutes is a good practice.

It is best to determine intuitively how much to take. For example, two to five drops can be a good starting point. You might also try dowsing with a pendulum. Figure 6–1 can be used to determine the number of drops to take. We have also found that taking a small number of drops at frequent intervals gives a more potent effect than taking a larger quantity of drops once or twice. If you are taking an essence in order to acquaint yourself with the properties of a gemstone, however, once is often sufficient. Another practice you can follow on an ongoing basis is to take the essence or water fifteen to twenty minutes after meals so that it becomes a part of your daily routine.

It is possible to become overcharged with a gem essence. Watch for any signs of spaciness, dizziness, or other symptoms of discomfort that arise when you take the essence.

GEM ESSENCE FOR CLIENTS

We use gem essences with clients at the beginning of a healing session, and sometimes as a session in itself when the client wishes to use the essences on an ongoing basis. Here are the steps we follow:

1. Before beginning the process take an essence that balances you and helps you to release your personal will.

2. Hold the client's sending hand in your receiving hand, and hold the pendulum in your sending hand. Both of you should breathe deeply, relax, and center. Affirm that you are finding the essence that is for the highest good of the client at this time. The client can affirm openness to Higher Guidance.

3. Choose an essence with the client (see figures 6–3 through 6–8).

   a. Use a chart in the form of a circle or an arc and ask the pendulum to "Point to the essence that the client needs for his/her highest good at this time." Hold the pendulum over the center point of the circle, or the midpoint of the baseline of the arc.

   b. You can put your bottles in groups and ask, "Is there an essence in this group that the client needs for his/her highest good at this time?"

   c. Honor your intuitive insights about what the client needs, or what the client feels he or she needs.

4. Double check your choice by placing the essence bottle in the client's receiving hand, and asking the pendulum, "Is this the essence needed at this time?" Note the strength of the "yes" (see figure 6–2).

5. It is possible to combine gem essences. Ask your pendulum, "Point to another essence needed at this time on this chart," or "Is there any other essence needed at this time?" Have client hold the combination(s) of essences and ask, "Is this the most appropriate combination of essences at this time?"

6. Once you have determined the essence(s), you can determine the timing and the number of drops (see figure 5). With your pendulum ask the following questions:

   a. "Is the essence to be taken now, for one time only?"

   b. If the answer is no, use an arc and ask the pendulum to show you the number of days the essence is to be taken.

   c. If you or the client are to take the essence whenever needed, we have found it effective to take the essence when the need arises, and then every ten or fifteen minutes until a sense of balance returns. Usually two or three times is sufficient.

    d.   Use the same arc and ask to be shown the number of drops to be taken at one time.

    e.   If more than one essence is to be taken sequentially, allow a minimum of fifteen minutes between essences.

7.   Share with the client the purpose of the essence and the appropriate affirmations. Encourage a conscious focusing on the spiritual qualities of the stone whenever the essence is taken (see figure 6–9).

8.   After the client takes the essence, you can both sound the soul tone of the stone to amplify its effect, and sit quietly for a bit.

The effect of the gem essences can be minimized when you are consuming substances that alter the body's metabolism, such as coffee, alcohol, and cigarettes. For example, try not to follow the gem essence with a cup of coffee or a cigarette. Instead, take the gem essence and work with the affirmations as a special "mini-break" time of self-nurturing. Also, gem essences (unlike flower essences) can interfere with homeopathic remedies, so check with your homeopathic physician.

Figures 6–3 through 6–8 are charts for choosing gem essences with a pendulum. The stones are organized according to the chakra affinities in order to aid in choosing a stone to place on a particular chakra for healing work.

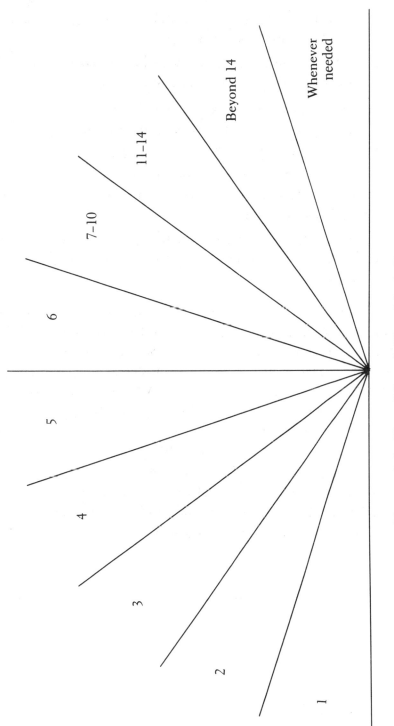

FIGURE 6–1. How Often & How Much Essence

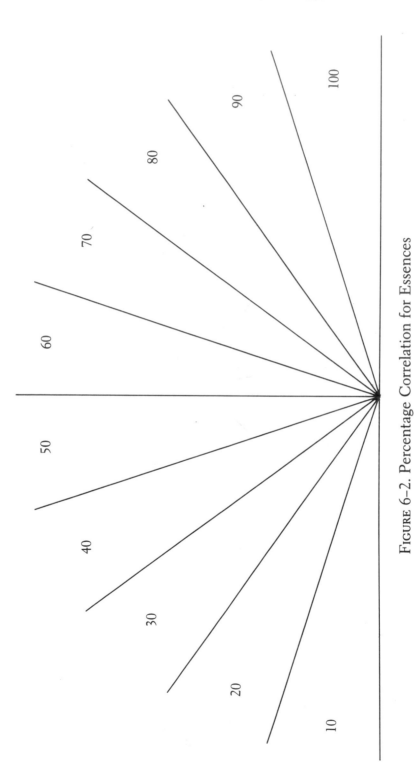

FIGURE 6–2. Percentage Correlation for Essences

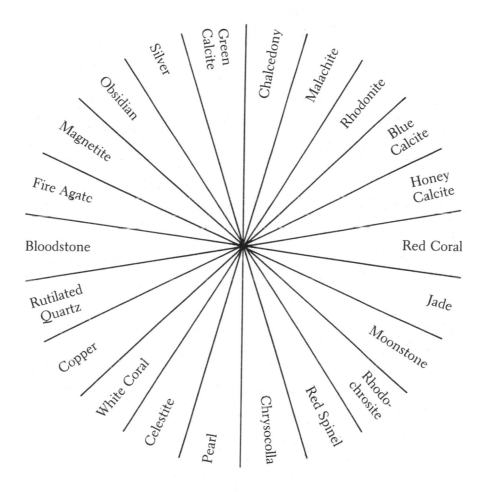

FIGURE 6–3. Clearing:
Gemstones and Essences—Root Through Throat Chakras

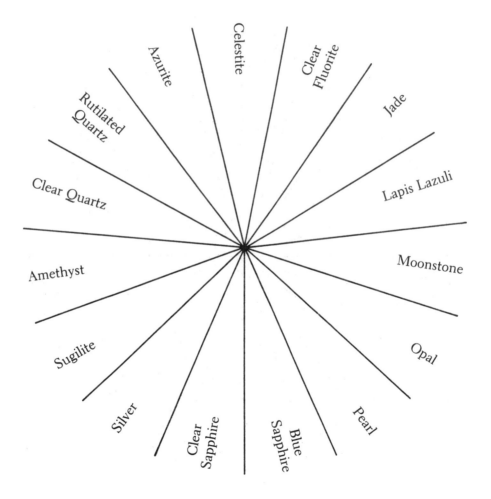

FIGURE 6-4. Clearing:
Gemstones and Essences—Third Eye and Crown Chakras

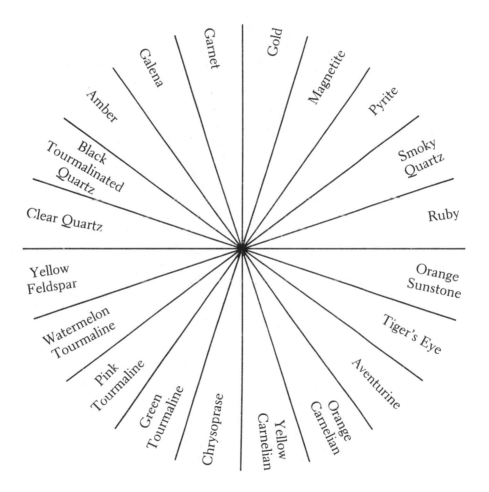

FIGURE 6–5. Building and Spiritual Expansion:
Gemstones and Essences—Root and Lower Abdomen Chakras

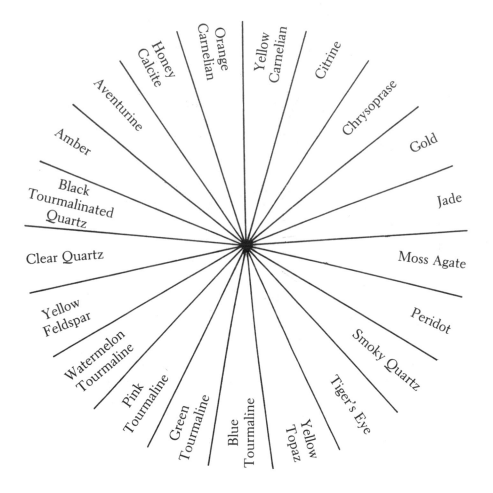

FIGURE 6–6. Building and Spiritual Expansion:
Gemstones and Essences—Solar Plexus Chakra

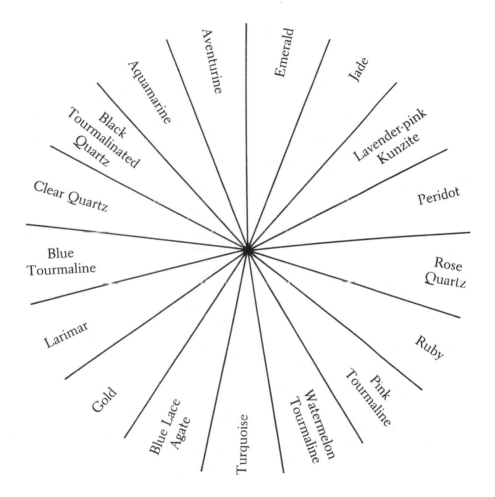

FIGURE 6-7. Building and Spiritual Expansion:
Gemstones and Essences—Heart and Throat Chakras

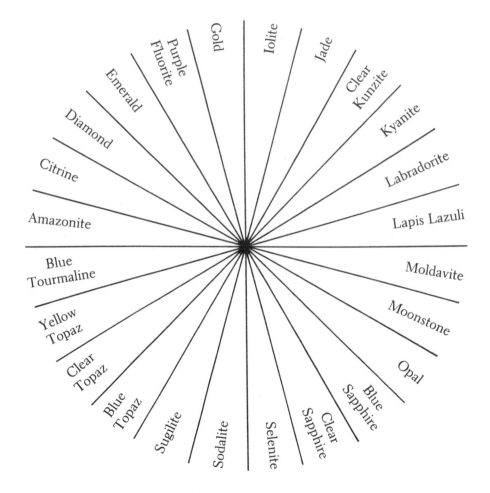

FIGURE 6–8. Building and Spiritual Expansion:
Gemstones and Essences—Third Eye and Crown Chakras

FIGURE 6–9.
Gemstone Affirmations and Soul Tones

Amazonite
A, A#
"I am protected by the Light as I move through transitions in my life, and I bless what I have accomplished."

Amber
C
"I build my physical vitality through lightness of spirit."

Amethyst
B
"I release all need for self-identity."

Aquamarine
G
"I am reassured and uplifted by the knowledge that my work is my love made visible."

Aventurine
E
"I expand my vision of who I can be."

Azurite
G#, G
"I find peace as I release emotional ties from the past."

Bloodstone
C#, C
"I affirm the power of my perseverance to see me through all situations."

Blue Lace Agate
G#
"I reflect calm inner certainty, as I speak with nonjudgment and discernment."

Green Calcite
D
"I release nervous tension and feel calm and relaxed."

Blue Calcite
E
"I affirm safety and peace during times of intensity."

Honey Calcite
D#
"I remain optimistic during times of intensity."

Orange Carnelian
D
"I find something positive to enjoy in every aspect of my life."

Yellow Carnelian
D#
"I enjoy the gifts of my everyday life with all my senses."

Celestite
G
"My mind is relaxed and open to connect with my Higher Guidance."

Chalcedony
D to E
"I trust the messages my feelings are giving me and I speak up for what I need."

Chrysocolla
F, F#, or G
"I listen to my heart to find and affirm my spiritual purpose."

Chrysoprase
D
"Completing one step at a time connects me with my inner roots and gives me a sense of continuity in my life."

Gemstone Affirmations and Soul Tones (cont'd)

Citrine
E
"I think and communicate clearly, synthesizing information from all levels of my being."

White Coral
G, G#
"I listen to that which is for my highest good and I release all else."

Red Coral
E
"I honor both my own unique path and the unique paths of others, by taking decisive action without judgment."

Diamond
B
"The purity of my actions reflects the moral code by which I live my life."

Emerald
F
"I joyfully give thanks for the abundance in my life."

Fire Agate
D
"I move forward with focus and direction and affirm that every moment is a new beginning."

Clear Fluorite
A#, A
"I release my personal will in order to purify my awareness."

Purple Fluorite
A,B
"As I merge with Divine Will, I find greater peace and illumination."

Galena
all tones
"I integrate my spiritual awareness by establishing my priorities and acting upon them."

Garnet
C
"I affirm my reservoir of inner strength and I act with practicality."

Iolite
B
"I open to greater personal and spiritual growth through communication with my soul."

Jade
E
"My body, mind, and spirit are in perfect balance."

Lavender-pink
Kunzite
F
"I live my life zestfully and creatively to the fullest."

Clear Kunzite
A
"I create to my highest capacity my vision of Light."

Kyanite
A#
"My physical body is a sacred temple built of pure Love."

Labradorite
B
"I now access the Akashic Records in order to expand my spiritual growth."

Lapis Lazuli
G#, A
"I seek the truth in understanding my experiences."

Gemstone Affirmations and Soul Tones (cont'd)

Larimar
G
"I fulfill my spiritual service in a way that is uniquely my own, to help others understand the unlimited nature of growth and knowledge."

Magnetite
C#
"I trust my abilities to accelerate change."

Malachite
E, F
"I have the courage and determination to work through all fear."

Moonstone
G#, A
"I value my emotional sensitivity, knowing that it is all right to feel what I am feeling."

Moldavite
B
"I go beyond limited thinking and receive the Unconditional Love present in other dimensions of the universe."

Moss Agate
E
"I initiate action to understand the spiritual dimension in all physical reality."

Obsidian
C, C#
"Letting go of my resistance to looking inward frees my personal power to bring about change."

Opal
A
"I am now free, independent, and creative, as I expand beyond perceived limitations from my past."

Pearl
A
"As I risk myself emotionally in order to heal, I am protected and nurtured."

Peridot
E
"Inner joy lights my way, and I share that joy with others."

Pyrite
C
"I open to receive additional life-force energy wherever it is needed."

Rhodochrosite
F
"I accept that I am truly a lovable being, and I forgive those who have forgotten that they are loved."

Rhodonite
D#
"I release my longing for the past as I find in every day something beautiful and new for me to appreciate."

Rose Quartz
F
"I delight in play and pleasure."

Ruby
F#, F
"I have the courage and strength to be who I truly am."

Gemstone Affirmations and Soul Tones (cont'd)

Rutilated Quartz all tones	"I can now see clearly beyond the illusions of my past."
Clear Sapphire A#	"I have faith and trust in the process of my growth toward the Light."
Blue Sapphire A	"Knowing that I am actively guided and supported in my growth toward the Light brings me peace."
Selenite A#, A	"I affirm my connection with my Spirit Guides."
Smoky Quartz C	"I find security in knowing that I can learn, whether I win or lose."
Sodalite A, A#	"My mind is calm and ordered so that I can concentrate with a singular focus."
Red Spinel E	"I strengthen my sense of self and my inner fulfillment as I complete my tasks in life."
Sugilite A#	"I am a Divine Manifestation of Love."
Orange Sunstone D#	"There is no limit to what I can do."
Tiger's Eye C#	"My belief in my purpose and my strength is the active foundation for my personal power."
Clear Topaz A#	"I joyfully expand the horizons of my spiritual understanding."
Yellow Topaz E	"I seek to comprehend the practical wisdom in all my experiences, and I manifest that wisdom."
Blue Topaz A	"I calmly accept the implications of my expanding spiritual understanding."
Black Tourmaline C	"I am emotionally safe and protected."
Black Tourmalinated Quartz all tones	"I am emotionally safe and protected."
Blue Tourmaline E	"Following the beat of my own drummer, I do what is right for me on my spiritual path, and I release the expectations of others."

Gemstone Affirmations and Soul Tones (cont'd)

Green Tourmaline E	"I let go of my inner expectations about how my life needs to be."
Pink Tourmaline D	"I accept you without judgment and without expectation."
Watermelon Tourmaline D#, E	"I calmly release my expectations of others."
Turquoise F#	"I am One with the Earth and I honor all life with love and respect."
Yellow Orthoclase Feldspar E, D#	"I move forward confidently on my path."

METALS

Copper D	"Life-force energy is now flowing smoothly throughout my body, giving me greater health and vitality."
Gold E	"I am actualizing my highest potential."
Silver D	"I am in harmony with my emotional body."

7 | More Dimensions in Gemstone Healing

To share in a healing process is to experience the awe, joy, and compassion of spiritual communion. The manner in which you experience the healing process, as well as how you utilize the stones in this work, determines how you are affected by them. In healing work you are "programming" or "focusing" the energy of the stones in a particular manner for a particular purpose.

In this chapter we explain some ways that you can work with one or two stones in healing, and how you can amplify a stone's energies with clear quartz crystal, gem essences, and sound. The role of the thymus gland in healing will also be clarified, so that you will know how to amplify the energy effect of gem jewelry worn over the heart. In preparation for our discussion of combining stones, we will return to our visual model of the healing process, which can also help us to understand the functioning of the thymus gland. Figures 7–5 and 7–6 are pendulum charts for the thymus gland stones mentioned in this book.

178

AMPLIFYING GEMSTONES WITH CLEAR QUARTZ CRYSTAL AND GEM ESSENCES

You can lay a stone on the body and amplify it in several ways using clear quartz crystal and gem essences. The following ideas are methods of healing through the amplification of life-force energies:

1. Glue or place a tiny stone onto a clear quartz crystal to amplify its energies.

2. Place a drop of the gem essence onto the termination of a clear quartz crystal and point it toward the stone on the body.

3. Utilize a treated crystal in place of a stone. The advantages are that you can often buy an essence such as diamond more inexpensively than you can buy the stone itself, and thus experience a wider variety of stones. Also, in our experience it takes less time to clean and clear quartz crystal by the salt-water method (as well as some other methods), than it does a gemstone. Some clients at times respond better to a treated crystal on the third eye than the stone itself. The disadvantage is that the energy seems a little weaker than that of the stone itself. Utilizing crystals with essences can give you more flexibility in your healing work.

4. Place the stone in a clear crystal grid and treat the crystals' terminations with the stone's essence. If you utilize the crystals without treating them, you get more "clear crystal energy" and less "stone energy." A *grid* is a specific pattern of stones, usually geometric in nature, that creates a vortex of energy.

5. If you wish to work on one area with more than one stone, you can infuse the energy of one stone, remove it, then place the second stone on the body. In this way you get an "undiluted dose" of a particular stone's energy with a magnified effect. If you are also utilizing treated crystals, remember to wash them off before adding another stone and its essence.

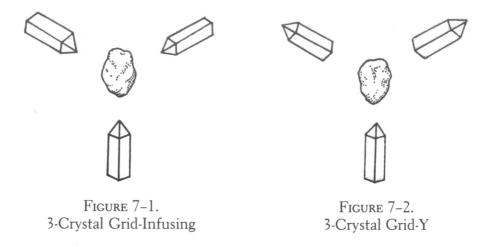

FIGURE 7–1.
3-Crystal Grid-Infusing

FIGURE 7–2.
3-Crystal Grid-Y

6. If you are utilizing a clear quartz crystal to work with the energy field above the body, you can put a drop of the stone's essence on the termination. However, if you rotate a treated crystal over a different kind of stone, the stone's qualities are diffused.

AMPLIFYING GEMSTONES WITH SOUND

Sound is a powerful amplifier for stones. Using the soul tone, either with your voice or a tuning fork, will amplify the spiritual purpose of the stone. You may have wondered about stones such as kyanite, which have a soul tone different from its visible color. You can receive life-force energy from any mineral, whether you are operating through its color or its soul tone. When you are working with the soul tone, the energies are of a more refined nature because the energy originates in the spiritual realm. When you are working with color, you are working with life-force energy that has been stepped down to a visible form. Both energies have their value in the healing process, and you enhance the capacities of a mineral if you operate from the spiritual as well as the visible level.

In general, optimal energy amplification occurs when the soul tone of a stone is within a half-tone of the personal chakra tone. For example, peridot (soul tone E) has an optimal placement on the solar plexus (D#, E) and the heart (F). When the range is within a whole tone there is slightly less amplification, but still an adequate balancing effect. When the discrepancy becomes greater, such as if you place jade (E) or citrine (E) on the third eye (G#, A, A#, B), an additional step is needed to maintain the integrity of the energy field. The easiest possibility is to follow the jade with a clear quartz crystal placed on the third eye. Clear quartz crystal has the capacity to integrate the energies into an overall balance. A second possibility is to create the soul tone and then the personal chakra tone. The chart of chakra affinities and soul tones of the stones at the end of Chapters 8 and 9 can be helpful here.

At any given time you can make a decision about how to focus the healing energy. In working with sound, particularly if you are working with tuning forks, it is best to utilize one tuning fork at a time. If you try to use two at a time, one tone will predominate. The other tone will lose its individual frequency and merge with the dominant tone, in a sympathetic resonance.

If you wish to work with a tone corresponding to a color, use that tone first, and follow it with the soul tone. We generally find the use of the soul tone to be sufficient.

If the client tones the soul tone of a particular stone, this also has a powerful effect because he or she is more consciously involved in the healing process.

ADDITIONAL SUGGESTIONS FOR USING INDIVIDUAL STONES FOR HEALING

When you work with one or two stones on the body at a time, you have more choices about where to place the stones for healing. In all examples, we ask the Mineral Deva or Higher Guidance to work with us, focusing the energy to the areas in need:

1. For self-healing you can place a stone on the third eye and direct its energies wherever needed. You can use hypoallergenic tape to secure the stone on the third eye so that you can either sit up or lie down. The third eye is able to interpret different kinds of input and then direct energy according to that input.

2. For self-healing hold a stone or take its essence and focus
   your intention on locating where in your body you are holding imbalanced energy. The stone acts as a radar device that
   locates and amplifies restricted energy where clearing needs
   to take place. Kyanite and sugilite, as well as other stones to
   which you may be attracted, can aid you in this process.

3. When working with others, scan the body with your sensing hand to locate imbalances, and intuitively decide where
   your energy work will have the greatest impact. Often this
   will be the area that is most out of balance. Hold the stone
   in your sending hand about a foot above the body and direct energy into the affected area.

4. You can also hold the stone in your sending hand above the
   body, and make clockwise circles until you have the sense
   that the area has received what it needs. This is the infusing position described in Chapter 3 as well as in *The Newcastle Guide to Healing with Crystals* (see figure 7–3).

   A clockwise circle can infuse a concentrated energy
   like a laser beam. Follow with counterclockwise circles, un-

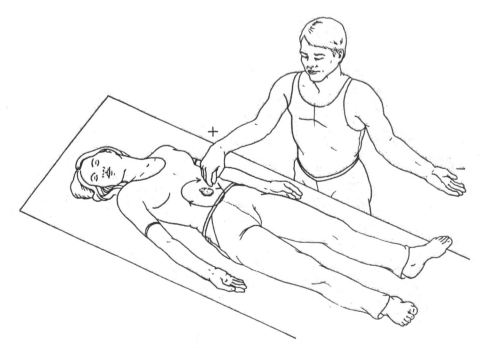

FIGURE 7–3. Clockwise Infusion.

til the area has received enough energy. Counterclockwise movements can infuse a more diffuse energy that spreads over a wider area.

THE FREQUENCY BAND—A MODEL

The healing process was described in Chapter 4 as dispersing dense, imbalanced energy, building balanced energy, and expanding into higher frequencies of energy. Also in Chapter 4 we introduced the model of a frequency band, which describes a gradual progression from left to right of denser to finer energy.

Clearing	Building and Infusing	Spiritual Expansion

FIGURE 7–4a. The Frequency Band

The clearing frequencies correspond in a greater degree to emotional and mental tension and stress. The building frequencies correspond to an increasingly finer level of energy that comes from infusing healthy, positive thoughts into the system. The spiritual expansion frequencies are focused neither on emotional pain nor mental imbalance. Rather, they encourage exploration and greater spiritual awareness.

Stones seem to have specialties within the frequencies of energy in which they work. Malachite, for example, clears the dense imbalance of fear and combines well with a number of stones. On the frequency band we would place it at the "clearing" end of our model. Opal is a catalyst that can open a dense area and infuse it with greater light.

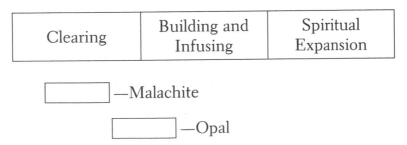

FIGURE 7–4b. Frequency Band.

Chrysoprase is an example of a stone that has a specific building function, working mainly on the etheric, emotional, and mental subtle bodies. It combines well with only a small number of stones, which indicates a very specialized range of functioning. By comparison, emerald, another green stone, is active on the emotional, mental, and spiritual subtle bodies. It seems to work at a higher frequency of energy. It also combines well with a number of stones, indicating a broader range of functioning.

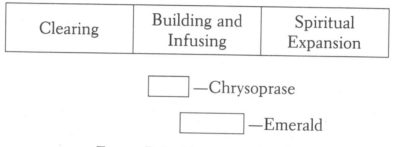

FIGURE 7–4c. Frequency Band.

Amazonite is an example of a stone that helps us make the transition from finite, separate beings on the emotional and mental levels to Infinite Beings that are part of All That Is. Labradorite does not work with personal growth, as amazonite can, as its specialized function is to help us understand the spiritual dimensions of our reality.

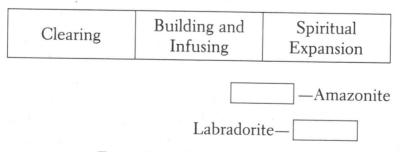

FIGURE 7–4d. Frequency Band.

Turquoise and moss agate are stones that have a similar function, in that they both can help you attune to the spiritual dimensions in the Kingdoms of Nature. They can also be utilized in a similar manner on the body. Turquoise is attuned to a slightly denser frquency than moss agate. We would illustrate turquoise and moss agae in this manner:

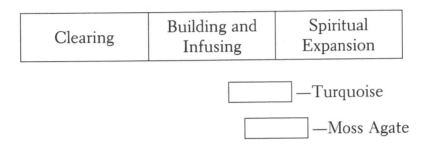

Clearing	Building and Infusing	Spiritual Expansion

☐ —Turquoise

☐ —Moss Agate

FIGURE 7–4e. Frequency Band.

This visual conceptualization may give you a means to interpret what you sense when you hold a stone or place it on the body. One application we have made of this model experientially is to observe that *stones which work with a similar frequency of density often combine well together.* For example, noticing whether a stone seems to disperse or build energy may give you clues about other stones that may be compatible. The layouts described in Chapters 8, 9, and 10 will illustrate compatible stone combinations, as well as their functioning at the different frequency levels.

Another observation we have made in using this model is that *optimal healing occurs when you balance the densest energy first.* Another way to express this concept is that stones working at higher frequencies will have a greater impact if the denser energies are balanced first. Relating some personal experiences may illustrate this idea.

Upon discovering some of the qualities of topaz in meditation, I was excited about trying the essence. If I was doubtful or unhappy and wanted to feel the uplifting inspiration of topaz, I would take the essence. It didn't seem to have much effect on me, however. But when I worked with rhodochrosite essence and it did help me remove my feelings of unhappiness, I could then follow it with topaz essence, and be more aware of its effects.

It is also our experience that we can move to higher levels without first clearing and balancing our energies. However, our physical bodies will still need just as much rest at night. But if we take time to clear and balance our energies first, our sleep is more restful and there is an accompanying sense of overall well-being and greater personal growth. Another way of stating this would be that *the higher frequencies of energy seem to integrate better with the subtle bodies when all of the bodies have been balanced.*

THE THYMUS GLAND

The frequency-band model can help you understand the stones which have an affinity with the thymus gland (see figure 7–4f). Stones with an affinity for the third eye, such as amazonite, work on the spiritual subtle body, helping you move from emotional and mental states of mind to a spiritual awareness. On the other hand, stones with an affinity for the thymus gland are catalysts on this same frequency level, helping you to *integrate the energy of your spiritual awareness into both your etheric subtle body and your physical body.*

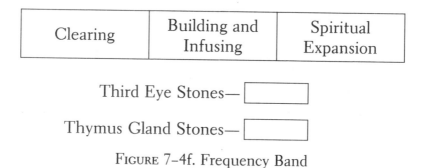

Clearing	Building and Infusing	Spiritual Expansion

Third Eye Stones—☐

Thymus Gland Stones—☐

FIGURE 7–4f. Frequency Band

The thymus gland and the heart chakra have separate locations on the body and separate but interrelated functions. The thymus gland *receives* spiritual life-force energies that come from our awareness and acceptance of the spiritual dimension in life, and transforms it for use in the etheric subtle body and physical vehicle. The primary function of the heart chakra is to *give* energy as Unconditional Love to others, although the heart chakra also receives spiritual energy and transforms it for use no the emotional/mental subtle bodies. Therefore it can be useful to work with stones on both the heart chakra and the thymus gland, to receive and transmit life-force energy on all levels of your being. When you seek to understand the level of physical balance in the body, the thymus gland can be an initial contact point. There are several ways that you can do this:

1. Scan the thymus gland area with your sensing hand and sense for any restrictions of life-force energy.

2. Hold a pendulum over the thymus gland and ask the pendulum to indicate the gland's strength.

3. Use a muscle-testing procedure to test the thymus gland's strength.[1] This requires two people:

    a. The client holds the left arm straight out to the side, parallel to the floor, with the elbow straight. The client then places the fingertips of the right hand midway between the throat and the line of the breasts, in the middle of the chest. This is the area of the thymus gland.

    b. Facing the client, the tester places the left hand on the client's shoulder and the right hand on the client's extended arm, above the wrist.

    c. On the count of three the client pushes his arm up and the tester presses down. If the thymus gland is strong, the arm should not move. If it is weak you will push the arm down easily. (If you repeat this test and have the client think of negative and then positive thoughts, you will notice that the thymus gland will test strong with the positive thoughts.)

    d. If there is physical imbalance, or a lack of positive thinking, the area may test weak.

If the gland has been dormant because the client has not been in contact with spiritual meaning or purpose in his or her life, it may take some time to activate the gland. Activating the gland can strengthen the immune system. This can be done in the following ways:

1.   Positive thinking is a necessity. Appreciate and affirm health in your physical body. Receive the Unconditional Love that pours into you from Nature and from other beings. Accept that there is more to life than the physical reality that you see. Discover and affirm your own spiritual purpose.

2.   Wearing stones at the thymus gland can help. Affirm the qualities of the jewelry when you put it on and ask that you receive its energies throughout the day.

3.   Place a stone on the thymus gland during healing sessions (see Chapters 8 and 9).

4.   Activate the gland with sound. You can use a tone that is between the heart and throat chakra tones. For example, my personal heart tone is F#, my thymus tone is G, and my throat is G#.

5.   When you are in the sunlight, consciously affirm that you are taking in the life-force energy of the sun for the health and well-being of your physical body.

6.   Tap the area lightly with your fingers up to about twenty-five times and then sense the energy of the area.

It is possible to overstimulate the thymus gland by giving it too much attention too quickly. Signs of overstimulation are jitteriness and feeling "hyped up." You can release an overcharge by mentally visualizing the energy at the thymus gland dispersing to all parts of your body. You can also place your receiving hand over the thymus and visualizing the energy moving out your sending hand. (This is the clearing position described in *The Newcastle Guide to Healing with Crystals*.)

Here is a listing of stones and metals that we have found to have an affinity for the thymus gland:

turquoise	amethyst
moss agate	clear quartz crystal
moldavite	rutilated quartz
amazonite	gold

Turquoise and moss agate have a primary affinity with the thymus gland, while the other stones have functions on other chakras as well. Figures 7–5 and 7–6 are arcs for pendulum dowsing thymus gland stones.

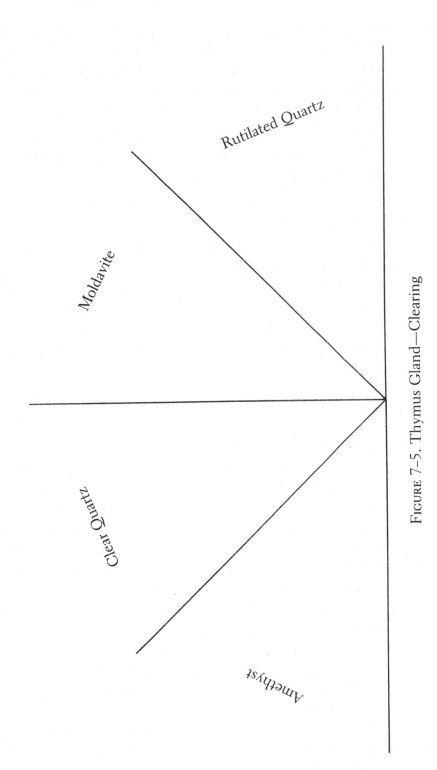

FIGURE 7–5. Thymus Gland—Clearing

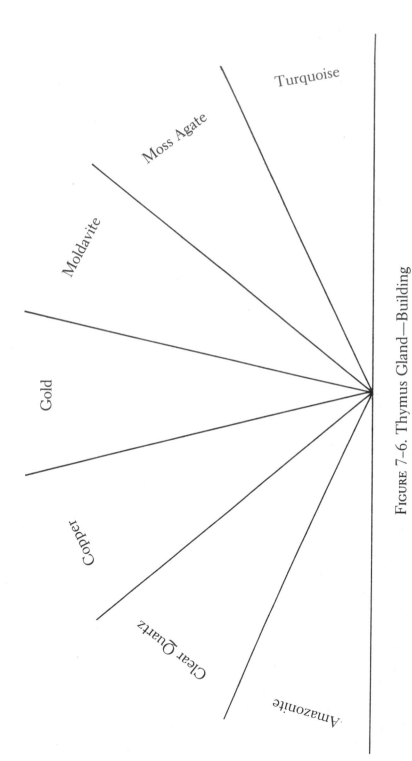

FIGURE 7–6. Thymus Gland—Building

8 | The Clearing Layouts

GEMSTONE LAYOUTS AS A TOOL FOR HEALING

When you work with a combination of stones, you can have a more thorough effect on your energy field. However, the compatibility of the stones becomes very important. The aim is to create a heightened and unified energy field rather than a diffusion of diverse frequencies. An important factor in combining stones is *how you personally attune with them in creating an energy field.*

In our work we have chosen to focus on the chakra system. By placing a stone on each chakra and the thymus gland, we create an "energy circuit" that affects all of the subtle bodies. It appears that by connecting the chakras, the energy created is greater than the sum of its parts. Small stones used in a pattern on a particular chakra have greater potency than when utilized singly, because of the current of energy that is created. We developed three criteria for the layouts.

The first criterion is the stones' affinity for a particular chakra. Stones that have an affinity for a specific chakra affect all of the subtle bodies more strongly. We experimented with

191

layouts using compatible stones but we placed them on chakras for which they did not have a primary affinity. We discovered that they effectively balanced the spiritual subtle bodies, but not necessarily the emotional and mental subtle bodies.

The Second criterion is compatibility of frequency. Stones with compatible frequencies are well attuned in the manner that they move energy, as well as the density of energy with which they work. This can create a unified flow that is very smooth. For example, we stated earlier that "clearing" stones that disperse denser energy are more likely to be compatible. Relating stones to an Element (See Chapter 4) is an attempt to describe how the energy of the stone moves. The "Earth" stones seem to slow down, focus, or stabilize energy, and therefore are often compatible in frequency.

Stones that are not well attuned can sometimes create uncomfortable sensations. A sign of incompatibility among stones on the body is feeling pressure or tingling in your hands.

In layouts where there is a compatibility of frequency at the spiritual subtle body level but not at other levels, one particular stone may serve as a unifying energy. The layout will not flow without that stone. In more highly compatible layouts, a stone can be removed and the layout will still flow. The layouts we have chosen to share are ones in which the stones seem highly compatible to us, so that you will have a beginning place to sense how to build your own layouts.

The third criterion relates to a compatibility of purpose. We have tried to describe an overall purpose for the layouts, and with some study you can see what each stone contributes. For example, tiger's eye can help you to feel your own power, and it combines well with ruby, which affirms courage and confidence.

Knowing groupings of minerals that work effectively together can give you a wider range of choices in how to approach a particular healing session.

CHOOSING AND WORKING WITH A LAYOUT

We often begin by choosing a stone intuitively for the third eye. You can ask what stone would be best and wait receptively for the answer, or you can dowse with a pendulum. The charts at the end of Chapter 6 can be helpful for this purpose. Next, choose a stone for the heart, solar plexus, or the most imbalanced chakra. The third-eye stone and the stones for imbalanced chakras will determine the nature of the layout. The other choices in the layout can be made according to the qualities of the stones involved, or what feels most appropriate on a given chakra. You can learn a lot, as we did, through placing the layouts on yourself and observing how they work. You can also choose according to the purpose and qualities of a particular layout.

It is possible to substitute *clear quartz crystal* for any stone in a layout. The crystal will maintain and amplify the qualities of the energy flow established by the other stones.

Depending on your own skills and training, there are two methods of working with the layout. One way is to place a layout on the client's body to balance the energy field, and to then work with other therapeutic skills. For example, if you are a counselor doing past-life therapy, you can utilize a layout that helps disperse blocked energy while you focus on the past-life process with your client.

The other method is to focus your energy primarily on the stones, while the client remains receptive to the healing energy. It is also possible to combine both methods together.

The layouts can both clear up problem areas and fine-tune your energy to be receptive to specific qualities. You may find it helpful to integrate clear quartz crystal in some manner as you work with the layouts, to help integrate these more specialized energies and amplify the overall balance of life-force energies. We will now review some ideas that were given in *The Newcastle Guide to Healing with Crystals* and also add to them:

1. Hold a clear quartz crystal in your sending hand, pointing toward the fingertips, and rotate four to twelve inches above the stone on each chakra, until each area has received enough energy.

    a. In a clearing layout we follow a two-step rotation. First *infuse* the energy of the stone, rotating the hand-held crystal *clockwise* over the stone on the chakra (see figure 8–1). Then change to the clearing position to open the flow of energy in the body. The clearing position involves holding the receiving hand over the chakra. Rotate the hand-held crystal *counterclockwise* down by your side (see figure 8–2).

b.   In a building or spiritual expansion layout we follow a different two-step rotation, first described in Chapter 7. First, we *infuse* the energy of the stone by rotating the crystal *clockwise* over the stone on the chakra, as in figure 8–1. Then we spread the energy over a larger area of the body by rotating *counterclockwise* over the chakra (see figure 8–3).

2.   Place a clear quartz crystal on each chakra and combine with either of the above two steps. (See figures 8–14 and 9–12 at the end of Chapters 8 and 9.) These figures illustrate the use of clear quartz crystals in grid patterns with gemstones.

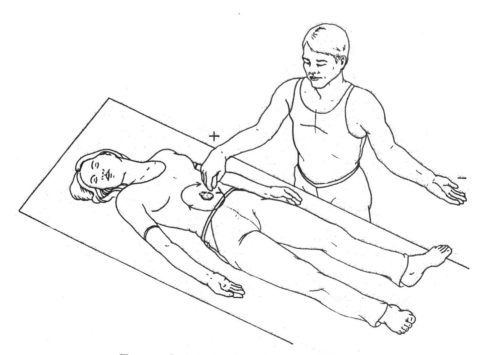

Figure 8–1. Infusing Energy of Stone.

FIGURE 8–2. Clearing Energy.

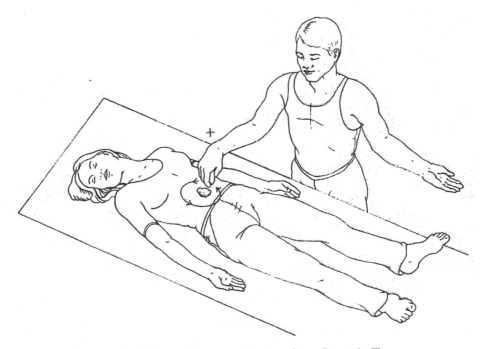

FIGURE 8–3. Spreading and Expanding Stone's Energy.

3.   Placing a clear quartz crystal grid around the body will also provide an overall balance and integration while you work with the gemstones (see figures 8–14 and 9–12).

4.   After you have infused the energy of the stone, you can integrate the energy field and complete the balancing by holding the crystal parallel to the body and pointing toward the head. Make three passes from the foot to the top of the head. The first pass, at about twelve inches or higher, balances the spiritual subtle bodies. The second pass, at four to twelve inches from the body, aligns the emotional and mental subtle bodies. The third pass, within a few inches of the body, integrates the etheric subtle body. You can also do this with the crystal pointing toward the body, which is more activating.

INTRODUCTION TO THE CLEARING LAYOUTS

These layouts have the common capacity to disperse imbalanced energy where flow has become restricted. A clearing layout may be the best choice when you are experiencing imbalanced emotions or thoughts, or you feel stuck in an area of your life and can't seem to break free. You can place a clearing layout on yourself at night to release that day's experiences and prepare for more complete rest. The stones can restore balance, peace, and a sense of priorities. Our clients have had dramatic results with the release of memories, past-life trauma, and other energy blocks through the use of these layouts.

Most of these layouts work well using amethyst at the crown. We have found that an amethyst point contributes the most dynamic flow of energy, although cluster or polished amethysts are also potent.

Effective thymus gland stones for clearing work would be *rutilated quartz, clear quartz, amethyst,* and *moldavite.* Moldavite, rutilated quartz, and to a lesser extent amethyst, are more likely to change the energy focus of the layout because they are a little more specific in their frequencies. You can utilize amethyst on the thymus when you have placed it at the crown. In other situations, clear quartz is a good choice. You can also omit the thymus gland stone if you wish, and still create a strong current of energy.

In reading the charts if there is more than one stone listed for a particular chakra, you can intuitively choose which one within that grouping is appropriate for your needs. However, the arrows and lines that connect particular stones indicate that these stones are only compatible with each other and not others in a group.

SIMPLE CLEARING LAYOUT—RUTILATED QUARTZ

The simplest clearing layout is rutilated quartz on all seven chakras and the thymus gland. Rutilated quartz is an excellent stone to begin with in learning about the clearing process. This layout can be intense and has a "let's-get-down-to-business" energy about it. There are a variety of ways this layout can be utilized. When you are working with a client and he or she is ready to take the next step or release something, the direct action of rutilated quartz may be needed. We have worked with rutilated quartz to begin the process of clearing particularly imbalanced areas, and followed it with a stone with more specific qualities relevant to the particular situation. This layout can clear and realign the chakras in preparation for the spiritually expanding layouts described in Chapter 10, as it has the effect of opening the energy pathways in all the subtle bodies.

Rutilated quartz can be substituted for other stones in the more active clearing layouts. With gentler stones, clear quartz may be more effective.

Root	Lower Abdomen	Solar Plexus	Heart	Throat	Third Eye	Crown
Rutilated Quartz	Rutilated Quartz	Rutilated Quartz	Rutilated Quartz	Rutilated Quartz	Rutilated Quartz	Rutilated Quartz

FIGURE 8–4. Simple Clearing Layout—Rutilated Quartz

SAFETY, GROUNDING, AND PROTECTION

Often, as you begin to explore personal issues in which changes are necessary, you may need to strengthen yourself with a sense of emotional safety. For example, this may be the case when you are learning to accept responsibility for your own health without engaging in self-judgment. When you are contemplating a location or relationship change, these stones can dissolve some of the anxiety and give a calm sense of groundedness. You can be reassured that you can move at a pace that is correct for you.

Root	Lower Abdomen	Solar Plexus	Heart	Throat	Third Eye	Crown
Smoky Quartz	Orange Carnelian	Moonstone	Chrysoprase Watermelon Tourmaline	Celestite	Clear Fluorite→ Blue Sapphire→	Amethyst Clear Sapphire

FIGURE 8–5. Safety, Grounding, and Protection.

CLEARING THE MIND OF MINOR UPSETS

This layout is excellent for relaxation at the end of a workday, when you wish to let go of the day's intensities. It is also powerful at the beginning of a healing session to help you shift into a healing mode. The action of this layout is calming and settling and helps to empty your mind of clutter. It can also prepare you for meditation. If you wish to work with jade on the third eye, try chrysocolla on the throat. With clear fluorite or celestite on the third eye, utilize celestite on the throat.

Root	Lower Abdomen	Solar Plexus	Heart	Throat	Third Eye	Crown
Black Tourmalinated Quartz Clear Fluorite	Green Calcite	Blue Calcite Moonstone Jade	Jade	Chrysocolla→ Celestite→ Celestite→	Jade Clear Fluorite Celestite	Amethyst

FIGURE 8–6. Clearing the Mind of Minor Upsets.

ACCEPTING PAINFUL FEELINGS, GENTLE CLEARING OF GRIEF

The first step in a healing process is often to accept that you have painful feelings about an experience. You may suppress these feelings, wishing they would go away. You may also become guilty, feeling that you haven't been practicing positive thinking, or you may feel weak in some way. These erroneous conclusions indicate that it is time to let go of self-judgment and acknowledge the pain so you can heal.

This layout can also help you deal with the grief of loneliness. Sometimes when you are unhappy, it may be because you are lonely. You can go through your daily activities without connecting with others in a meaningful way, giving rise to a sense of feeling separate.

These stones gently ask you to relax and nurture yourself, so you can let go of what needs to be released. If you wish to utilize sugilite on the third eye, place black tourmalinated quartz rather than bloodstone at the root. Chalcedony can be utilized with either layout at the solar plexus although blue calcite is the preferred stone.

Root	Lower Abdomen	Solar Plexus	Heart	Throat	Third Eye	Crown
Bloodstone Black Tourmalinated Quartz	Green Calcite	Blue Calcite Chalcedony	Rhodochrosite	Celestite	Moonstone Sugilite	Amethyst

Clear Fluorite	Green Calcite	Blue Calcite Chalcedony	Rhodochrosite	White Coral	Moonstone Pearl	Amethyst

FIGURE 8–7. Accepting Painful Feelings, Gentle Clearing of Grief.

BREAKING THROUGH LIMITATIONS AND FRUSTRATION/PAST LIVES

Sometimes the physical and emotional tension in your body is the result of holding yourself back because someone did not approve of you, or because you limited yourself in some way in order to survive. This layout, with its variations, is a useful one for breaking up conscious and subconscious limiting beliefs, especially where *fear* is involved. The stones can help fulfill a sense of understanding and confidence that comes from confronting and overcoming fear.

The stones in this layout support using jade on the third eye for past-life explorations. Past-life work with jade often proceeds very gently and with more safety. Other stones for past-life work include lapis, azurite, opal, and rutilated quartz. They are suggested in other layouts. Bloodstone and malachite emphasize strength and courage in breaking through limitations, and they can be utilized alone as a pair.

The first set of stones features compatible stones for jade and lapis on the third eye. In the second set, the first line shows stones that attune well with red coral on the solar plexus. The layout focuses more specifically on moving past fear of criticism. In the second line red spinel on the solar plexus strengthens the determination to complete a task despite fear that may hold you back. These stones in this set are not interchangeable, as indicated by the arrows.

Root	Lower Abdomen	Solar Plexus	Heart	Throat	Third Eye	Crown
Bloodstone Magnetite	Fire Agate	Chalcedony	Malachite	Celestite	Jade Lapis Lazuli	Amethyst

Root	Lower Abdomen	Solar Plexus	Heart	Throat	Third Eye	Crown
Rutilated Quartz→	Fire Agate→	Red Coral→	Malachite→	White Coral→	Rutilated Quartz→	Amethyst
Obsidian→	Fire Agate→	Red Spinel→	Malachite→	White Coral→	Lapis Lazuli→	Amethyst

FIGURE 8–8. Breaking Through Limitations and Frustrations/Past Lives

SUBCONSCIOUS CLEARING/PAST LIVES

These particular layouts show azurite on the third eye as a powerful subconscious clearer. Azurite, with the supporting stones, can give a sense of new awareness, as well as the peace that comes from emotional healing. This layout could also be utilized for dream dialogues. In the group with rhodochrosite on the heart, you should work with white coral at the throat, if you wish to utilize chalcedony on the lower abdomen. Fire agate on the lower abdomen is compatible with celestite on the throat.

Root	Lower Abdomen	Solar Plexus	Heart	Throat	Third Eye	Crown
Bloodstone Magnetite	Fire Agate Chalcedony	Chalcedony Malachite	Malachite	Chrysocolla	Azurite	Amethyst
Bloodstone	Chalcedony Fire Agate	Malachite	Rhodochrosite	White Coral Celestite	Azurite	Amethyst

FIGURE 8–9. Subconscious Clearing of Past Lives.

ANGER AND RESENTMENT/PAST LIVES

This layout, with its variations, is perhaps the most cathartic in the quality of its energy. It is therefore well-suited to releasing *anger* and *resentment*. You may have held onto anger for a while when you were hurt. It seems that perhaps the other person will be punished by your anger, although ultimately you suffer the most. The active dispersing qualities of this layout help you to acknowledge and release the tension of buried anger and resentment. This release is important, particularly with regards to health and parental issues, in which you may be unaware of the anger that is still there. We have encouraged clients to express that anger verbally, or through a sound or tone, or by breathing the anger up and out of the body. Awareness and understanding can help you come to terms with the past on a conscious level. The fiery nature of these stones affirms that you are free to be who you truly are.

This layout also supports rutilated quartz, opal, and lapis on the third eye for past-life work. All three stones work with amethyst at the crown, but only opal and rutilated quartz can work with iolite at the crown. If you wish to utilize obsidian on the root, it is best to work with rutilated quartz or lapis rather than opal on the third eye. The top row of stones is the most active. Substituting bloodstone, red spinel, or lapis reduces the intensity.

Root	Lower Abdomen	Solar Plexus	Heart	Throat	Third Eye	Crown
Obsidian	Fire Agate	Malachite	Rhodochrosite	Celestite	Rutilated Quartz\	Amethyst
Rutilated Quartz	Bloodstone	Red Spinel		White Coral	Opal→	Iolite
Bloodstone					Lapis Lazuli	

FIGURE 8–10. Anger and Resentment/Past Lives

FORGIVENESS/OPENING THE HEART

This layout includes some of the stones involved in other release work and is also active and cathartic. You can focus on the qualities of Unconditional Love and forgiveness, which are radiated by rhodochrosite and further defined by the various other stones.

Once you have acknowledge and accepted anger, you need to forgive and open your heart again. One of the ways to heal a blow to your self-esteem is to give yourself support through self-affirmation and especially self-acceptance. This layout gives many affirming qualities and is useful when you need only not to be aware of past influences but to heal the past as well. If you wish to work with fire agate, utilize celestite on the throat. Blue sapphire on the third eye works best with clear sapphire on the crown, but does not combine as well with amethyst. Lapis on the third eye works with amethyst, rather than clear sapphire.

Root	Lower Abdomen	Solar Plexus	Heart	Throat	Third Eye	Crown
Bloodstone	Fire Agate Chalcedony	Malachite Red Coral	Rhodochrosite	Celestite White Coral	Blue Sapphire ↔ Lapis Lazuli ↔	Clear Sapphire Amethyst
Magnetite Bloodstone	Fire Agate	Red Spinel	Rhodochrosite	White Coral	Opal	Amethyst

FIGURE 8–11. Forgiveness/Opening the Heart

REINTEGRATION AFTER A CLEARING LAYOUT

Sometimes after balancing the energy flow with the clearing layouts, there can be a sense of vulnerability that accompanies the change and the new awareness. There are several ways that you can reintegrate the new energy patterns into the total energy system:

1.   Place a clear quartz crystal on each chakra as described in *The Nescastle Guide to Healing with Crystals*.

2.   Utilize one of the infusing layouts. You or the client can mentally repeat the appropriate healing affirmations.

3.   Find a way to infuse the energy of the color *green*. You or the client can breathe green, or visualize being in the woods or another green environment.

4.   Place a stone on the heart or the solar plexus and affirm its building qualities. Rhodochrosite or one of the green stones works well for this purpose.

5.   Treat each of seven crystals with one of the essences utilized in the layout. Place these crystals pointing out in a Star of David at the crown, with the crown crystal in the center. You can hold a clear quartz crystal and rotate it counterclockwise over the Star of David until the energy is heightened. The client can affirm that Higher Guidance is helping to reintegrate the new understanding for healing (see figure 8–12).

6.   At the completion of past-life work, *iolite* can be placed in the center of the Star of David grid of treated crystals mentioned above (see figure 8–13). The client can dialogue with his or her Soul to receive positive qualities which were developed in past lives to use for healing at this time.

FIGURE 8–12.
Crown Layout—Clearing

FIGURE 8–13.
Crown Layout—Iolite

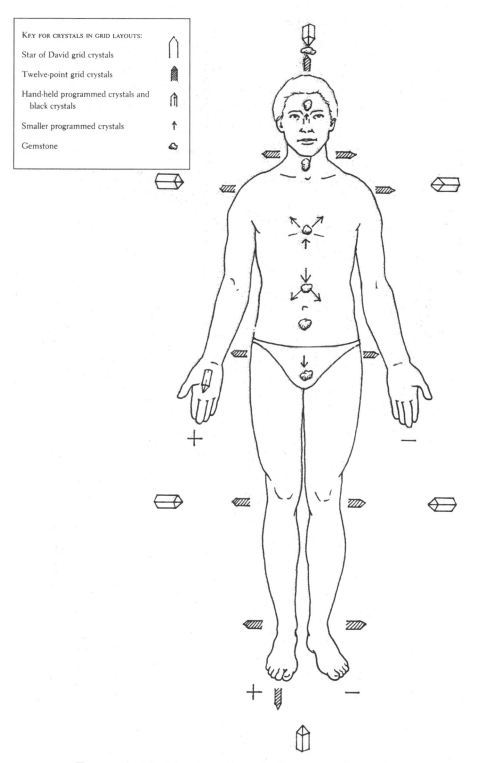

Key for crystals in grid layouts:

Star of David grid crystals

Twelve-point grid crystals

Hand-held programmed crystals and
   black crystals

Smaller programmed crystals

Gemstone

Figure 8–14. Clearing Crystal Gemstone Layout.

FIGURE 8–15. Gemstone Chakra Affinities for Clearing

ROOT	LOWER ABDOMEN	SOLAR PLEXUS	HEART	THROAT	THIRD EYE	CROWN
Bloodstone, 1	Bloodstone, 1	Bloodstone, 2	Green Calcite, 2	Celestite, 1	Amethyst, 2	Amethyst, 1
Fire Agate, 2	Green Calcite, 1	Blue Calcite, 1	Chrysocolla, 2	Chrysocolla, 1	Azurite, 1	Clear Fluorite, 1
Clear Fluorite, 1	Chalcedony, 1	Honey Calcite, 1	Jade, 1	White Coral, 1	Celestite, 1	Clear Sapphire, 1
Magnetite, 1	Fire Agate, 1	Chalcedony, 1	Malachite, 1		Clear Fluorite, 1	Silver, 2
Obsidian, 1	Malachite, 2	Red Coral, 1	Pearl, 2		Jade, 1	Sugilite, 2
Silver, 1	Obsidian, 1	Jade, 1	Rhodochrosite, 1		Lapis Lazuli, 1	
	Rhodonite, 1	Malachite, 1	Silver, 1		Moonstone, 1	
	Silver, 1	Moonstone, 1			Opal, 1	
		Obsidian, 2			Pearl, 1	
		Rhodochrosite, 2			Blue Sapphire, 1	
		Rhodonite, 1			Clear Sapphire, 1	
		Red Spinel, 1			Silver, 1	
					Sugilite, 1	

ALL CHAKRA AFFINITIES
Clear Quartz
Rutilated Quartz

NO CHAKRA AFFINITIES
Copper

THYMUS GLAND CLEARING
Amethyst, 1
Clear Quartz, 1
Moldavite, 1
Rutilated Quartz, 1

KEY
1—Primary chakra affinity
2—Secondary chakra affinity

FIGURE 8–16. Gemstone Soul Tones for Clearing

ROOT	LOWER ABDOMEN	SOLAR PLEXUS	HEART	THROAT	THIRD EYE	CROWN
Bloodstone, C#, C	Bloodstone, C#, C	Bloodstone, C#, C	Green Calcite, D	Celestite, G	Amethyst, B	Amethyst, B
Fire Agate, D	Green Calcite, D	Blue Calcite, E	Chrysocolla, G, F, F#	Chrysocolla, G, F, F#	Azurite, G#, G	Clear Fluorite, A#, A
Clear Fluorite, A#, A	Chalcedony, E, D	Honey Calcite, D#	Jade, E	White Coral, G, G#	Celestite, G	Clear Sapphire, A#
Magnetite, C#	Fire Agate, D	Chalcedony, E, D	Malachite, E, F		Clear Fluorite, A#, A	Silver, D
Obsidian, C#, C	Malachite, E, F	Red Coral, E	Pearl, A		Jade, E	Sugilite, A#
Silver, D	Obsidian, C#, C	Jade, E	Rhodochrosite, F		Lapis Lazuli, G#, A	
	Rhodonite, D#	Malachite, E, F	Silver, D		Moonstone, G#, A	
	Silver, D	Moonstone, G#, A			Opal, A	
		Obsidian, C#, C			Pearl, A	
		Rhodochrosite, F			Blue Sapphire, A	
		Rhodonite, D#			Clear Sapphire, A#	
		Red Spinel, E			Silver, D	
					Sugilite, A#	

THYMUS GLAND CLEARING
Amethyst, B
Clear Quartz
Moldavite, B
Rutilated Quartz

ALL CHAKRA AFFINITIES
Clear Quartz
Rutilated Quartz

NO CHAKRA AFFINITIES
Copper, D

FIGURE 8-17. Summary of Clearing Layouts

PURPOSE	ROOT	LOWER ABDOMEN	SOLAR PLEXUS	HEART	THROAT	THIRD EYE	CROWN
Simple Clearing—(Rutilated Quartz)	Rutilated Quartz	Rutilated Quartz	Rutilated Quartz	Rutilated Quartz	Rutilated Quartz	Rutilated Quartz	Rutilated Quartz
Safety, Grounding, Protection	Smoky Quartz	Orange Carnelian	Moonstone	Chrysoprase Watermelon Tourmaline	Celestite	Clear Fluorite→ Blue Sapphire→	Amethyst Clear Sapphire
Clearing the Mind of Minor Upsets	Black Tourmalinated Quartz Clear Fluorite	Green Calcite	Blue Calcite Moonstone Jade	Jade	Chrysocolla→ Celestite→ Celestite→	Jade Clear Fluorite Celestite	Amethyst
Accepting Painful Feelings; Gentle Clearing of Grief	Bloodstone Black Tourmalinated Quartz Clear Fluorite	Green Calcite Green Calcite	Blue Calcite Chalcedony Blue Calcite Chalcedony	Rhodochrosite Rhodochrosite	Celestite White Coral	Moonstone Sugilite Moonstone Pearl	Amethyst Amethyst

FIGURE 8–17. Summary of Clearing Layouts

	Bloodstone / Magnetite	Fire Agate	Chalcedony	Malachite	Celestite	Jade / Lapis Lazuli	Amethyst
Breaking Through Limitations and Frustrations/ Past Lives	Bloodstone Magnetite	Fire Agate	Chalcedony	Malachite	Celestite	Jade Lapis Lazuli	Amethyst
	Rutilated Quartz→ Obsidian→	Fire Agate→ Fire Agate→	Red Coral→ Red Spinel	Malachite→ Malachite→	White Coral→ White Coral→	Rutilated Quartz→ Lapis Lazuli→	Amethyst
Subconscious Clearing/Past Lives	Bloodstone Magnetite	Fire Agate Chalcedony	Chalcedony Malachite	Malachite	Chrysocolla	Azurite	Amethyst
	Bloodstone	Chalcedony Fire Agate	Malachite	Rhodochrosite	White Coral Celestite	Azurite	Amethyst
Anger and Resentment/Past Lives	Obsidian	Fire Agate	Malachite	Rhocochrosite	Celestite	Rutilated Quartz ＼	Amethyst
	Rutilated Quartz Bloodstone	Bloodstone	Red Spinel		White Coral	Opal→ Lapis Lazuli	Iolite
Forgiveness/Opening the Heart	Bloodstone	Fire Agate Chalcedony	Malachite Red Coral	Rhodochrosite	Celestite White Coral	Blue Sapphire→ Lapis Lazuli↔	Clear Sapphire Amethyst
	Magnetite Bloodstone	Fire Agate	Red Spinel	Rhodochrosite	White Coral	Opal	Amethyst

9 | The Building Layouts

INTRODUCTION TO THE BUILDING LAYOUTS

Building layouts help you to affirm who you are and to move toward new possibilities in your personal growth. Clearing layouts are effective when a more intense degree of pain is involved. Building layouts are effective with less intense pain, and with the cultivation of spiritual qualities such as belief in your purpose. You can incorporate building layouts into your practice of affirmations. The stones will add their energy to your particular affirmations. Or you can work with the specific affirmations for individual stones to amplify their effect on your energy system. A layout can be placed on the body after a massage or other release work to strengthen new patterns of thought-energy.

The stones have been combined so that they are most attuned to one another, which is why there are several similar layouts. They all give slightly different energy effects on the body, depending on the spiritual qualities of the stones involved.

The "Element" layouts (Earth, Water, Fire, and Air) were named according to the correspondence of the quality of move-

210

ment in the layouts to an Element of Nature. We have experimented with several ways of integrating the qualities of these "Element" layouts with other healing practices:

1. If you work with guided imagery, ask what the client visualizes when he or she "goes to a quiet place to relax." If the client goes up to the top of a mountain, for example, you might utilize the "Air" layout and incorporate additional images of birds, clouds, soaring, wind, etc.

2. Determine what Elements and qualities particular music reminds you of, and play that music while you or the client attune with the layout. For example, Beethoven's Symphony No. 5 gets right to the heart of the Fire layout, and Dexter and Bearns' *Golden Voyage* series is a natural for the Earth layout.

3. We have collected information on our clients' sun, moon, and rising signs, as well as predominant and missing Elements in the astrological natal chart, to determine any affinities for a particular Element. Our observations have been fascinating but not definitive, so we make no generalizations. However, you may enjoy further study in correlating your own perceptions of Elements, stones, and astrology.

As in the clearing layouts, arrows indicate stones that are compatible and cannot be interchanged with another in that group. Otherwise, stones listed in each chakra grouping are interchangeable with one another.

Clear quartz is an excellent crown stone for any of these layouts and can also be placed on the thymus gland. Other possible thymus gland stones will be listed in the layout descriptions. Larimar is listed first when it is the throat stone of choice. However, because larimar is hard to obtain, blue lace agate (2) is often a good second choice. The name yellow orthoclase feldspar has been shortened to yellow feldspar for brevity.

The layouts are organized into four groupings: focusing on the present, emotional balance, mental balance, and taking action for change.

FOCUSING ON THE PRESENT—EARTH

These stones amplify the qualities of stability and centeredness which allow you to accept where you are and bring out your best in any situation. This layout will slow you down if you have a tendency to race through your days, enabling you to better calm and focus your mind. You may develop a greater sensitivity and enjoyment of your surroundings, as well as a greater ability to live in the present. This layout will also help you cultivate the qualities of inner sensitivity and patience, learn to take one step at a time, and finish what you start. Compatible thymus gland stones are *turquoise* and *amazonite*.

Root	Lower Abdomen	Solar Plexus	Heart	Throat	Third Eye	Crown
Garnet	Orange Carnelian→ Orange Carnelian→ Chrysoprase→	Chrysoprase Yellow Carnelian Aventurine	Jade	Blue Lace Agate	Sodalite Jade	Blue Kyanite

FIGURE 9–1. Focusing on the Present—Earth.

FOCUSING ON THE PRESENT—BEGINNING AGAIN

Often when you have undergone a release process which involves a change of perception, it feels as if your old familiar security blanket of beliefs is pulled out from under you. At this time you need to re-establish a sense of stability, realizing that you are now different than you were before. You can help to establish balance by focusing on the present and on new possibilities of who you can become.

This layout includes stones which can help you release inner expectations and trust in your new beginnings. In our practice we have noticed that during a series of sessions, a particularly strong cathartic session might require a gentler healing energy. Its energy can be helpful as you begin again after the acceptance of a loss or move of any kind. Its energy is reassuring and safe, and focuses on taking one step at a time. Rhodonite is compatible with chrysoprase or chalcedony on the solar plexus. If you wish to utilize green tourmaline on the solar plexus, place watermelon tourmaline on the lower abdomen. *Turquoise* is a compatible thymus gland stone.

Root	Lower Abdomen	Solar Plexus	Heart	Throat	Third Eye	Crown
Black Tourmalinated Quartz Bloodstone	Rhodonite→ Rhodonite→ Watermelon Tourmaline	Chrysoprase Chalcedony Green Tourmaline	Rhodochrosite	Celestite	Blue Sapphire	Clear Quartz

FIGURE 9–2. Focusing on the Present—Beginning Again.

EMOTIONAL BALANCE—WATER

These stones can aid you in accepting and affirming yourself *as you are*. There is a receptive, flowing quality to the energy that encourages you to open to life's experiences and enjoy them without expectations. You may also receive a heightened appreciation of your feeling nature and of beauty in all forms.

Rose quartz is compatible with all three third eye stones. Combine lavender-pink kunzite with sugilite or blue sapphire. Emerald is only compatible with moonstone in this layout. Compatible thymus gland stones are *turquoise* and *moldavite*.

Root	Lower Abdomen	Solar Plexus	Heart	Throat	Third Eye	Crown
Smoky Quartz	Aventurine	Green Tourmaline	Rose Quartz Lavender-pink Kunzite↗ Emerald→	Aquamarine	Sugilite Blue Sapphire Moonstone	Clear Quartz

FIGURE 9–3. Emotional Balance—Water.

EMOTIONAL BALANCE—ACCEPTING FEELINGS DURING CHANGE

The energy of this variation of the Water layout has a more accelerated movement toward change. If you are emotionally sensitive and tend to doubt yourself easily, these stones provide a gently reassuring but persistent encouragement to make those changes. *Turquoise* and *moss agate* can be placed on the thymus gland.

Root	Lower Abdomen	Solar Plexus	Heart	Throat	Third Eye	Crown
Magnetite Orange Sunstone Tiger's Eye	Aventurine	Yellow Feldspar Green Tourmaline	Emerald	Blue Lace Agate Aquamarine White Coral	Moonstone	Clear Fluorite Clear Quartz

FIGURE 9–4. Emotional Balance—Accepting Feelings During Changes.

EMOTIONAL BALANCE—OVERSENSITIVITY

This layout can aid those of you who are highly sensitive emotionally and easily influenced by the troubles of others. The stones can help you detach emotionally from taking unnecessary responsibility for others. You can develop the ability to move through your day with less effort and emotional intensity and more equanimity and balance.

Appropriate thymus gland stones are *turquoise* and *moldavite.*

Root	Lower Abdomen	Solar Plexus	Heart	Throat	Third Eye	Crown
Smoky Quartz	Green Tourmaline	Moonstone	Jade Watermelon Tourmaline	Blue Lace Agate	Jade	Clear Quartz

FIGURE 9–5. Emotional Balance—Oversensitivity.

EMOTIONAL BALANCE—RELEASING EXPECTATIONS

This layout features the tourmaline family. Its emphasis is on strengthening your sense of safety, while at the same time encouraging you to release unrealistic expectations of others in close relationships. This layout may give you insight on how to be clear about your needs without demanding that they be met. You may feel an increased understanding for the other person, as well as an increased trust in the process of growth for both of you.

Turquoise and *moldavite* are compatible thymus gland stones.

Root	Lower Abdomen	Solar Plexus	Heart	Throat	Third Eye	Crown
Black Tourmalinated Quartz	Watermelon Tourmaline	Green Tourmaline	Pink Tourmaline	Aquamarine	Moonstone	Clear Quartz

FIGURE 9–6. Emotional Balance—Releasing Expectations.

MENTAL BALANCE—AIR

The energy quality of these stones is light and uplifting. This layout can provide an expanded perspective which helps connect your conscious understanding to spiritual wisdom. Its focus is on broadening your knowledge of who you are in a joyful manner, and so it is well suited to working with affirmations. *Moss agate* and *moldavite* are compatible thymus gland stones.

Root	Lower Abdomen	Solar Plexus	Heart	Throat	Third Eye	Crown
Amber	Amber	Peridot	Emerald	Larimar	Clear Topaz	Diamond
Orange Sunstone	Yellow Feldspar Pink Tourmaline	Citrine		Blue Lace Agate		Clear Fluorite

FIGURE 9–7. Mental Balance—Air.

MENTAL BALANCE—MANIFESTING YOUR WISDOM

This variation of the Air layout focuses on practically applying your creative wisdom. There is more "energy impetus" in this layout to put your ideals into practice in some manner. An appropriate thymus gland stone is *moss agate*.

Root	Lower Abdomen	Solar Plexus	Heart	Throat	Third Eye	Crown
Tiger's Eye Orange Sunstone	Orange Carnelian	Blue Tourmaline Jade	Peridot	Aquamarine	Yellow Topaz Citrine	Diamond

Figure 9–8. Mental Balance—Manifesting Your Wisdom.

MENTAL BALANCE—CLARITY OF MIND

With their strong yellow vibrations, these stones combine to balance the mental subtle body, particularly the conscious, decision-making mind. Those of you who do a great deal of mental work during the day may find that this layout both relaxes you and restores and affirms your clarity. You might make this layout part of a relaxing break when you are working on an extended project that involves problem solving and concentration. These stones can strengthen your sense of timing to help you clarify when to act and when to gather information. Larimar is the throat stone in this layout. However, because it is rare, we suggest aquamarine instead, with citrine on the third eye, or blue lace agate with sodalite on the third eye. Stones for the thymus gland are *turquoise* and *moss agate*.

Root	Lower Abdomen	Solar Plexus	Heart	Throat	Third Eye	Crown
Amber	Yellow Feldspar	Citrine	Jade	Larimar→ Aqua-marine→ Blue Lace Agate→	Citrine Citrine Sodalite	Diamond

Figure 9–9. Mental Balance—Clarity of Mind.

TAKING ACTION FOR CHANGE—FIRE

The quality of energy in this stone combination is fiery and intense, generating in you the desire to get moving in your life. This layout can also encourage an increased confidence in your creative abilities. You may find yourself more optimistic and excited about your life and ready for new challenges. Turquoise and moss agate are compatible thymus gland stones.

Root	Lower Abdomen	Solar Plexus	Heart	Throat	Third Eye	Crown
Tiger's Eye	Orange Carnelian	Amber	Ruby	Larimar	Opal→	Clear Sapphire
	Amber	Peridot	Peridot	Aquamarine	Blue Sapphire→	Clear Sapphire
		Citrine		Blue Lace Agate	Lapis Lazuli→	Diamond

FIGURE 9–10. Taking Action for Change—Fire.

TAKING ACTION FOR CHANGE—MANIFESTING YOUR GOALS

Here we give three different layouts that are similar in frequency. They center around the theme of mobilizing your will to affirm your purpose. In the first layout, lapis on the third eye gives steadiness and helps build self-reliance. Diamond strengthens your desire to do what is right. In the second grouping, clear kunzite fires you up to manifest your vision. In the final combination opal affirms your freedom to be creative, and sugilite affirms your uniqueness.

Each layout features different stones on the solar plexus. In the first layout, jade and citrine give mental balance and strengthen clarity of purpose. In the second grouping yellow feldspar adds a sense of timing and warm enthusiasm to the motivation of kunzite. In the final combination the tourmalines and opal stress your appreciation of your unique contribution. *Turquoise* on the thymus gland is compatible with all three layouts.

Root	Lower Abdomen	Solar Plexus	Heart	Throat	Third Eye	Crown
Magnetite Tiger's Eye	Green Tourmaline	Jade Citrine	Peridot	Blue Lace Agate Aqua-marine	Lapis Lazuli Diamond	Clear Quartz

FIGURE 9–11a. Taking Action for Change—Manifesting Your Goals.

Root	Lower Abdomen	Solar Plexus	Heart	Throat	Third Eye	Crown
Magnetite Tiger's Eye	Watermelon Tourmaline	Yellow Feldspar	Ruby Peridot	Blue Lace Agate	Clear Kunzite	Clear Quartz

FIGURE 9–11b. Taking Action for Change—Manifesting Your Goals.

Root	Lower Abdomen	Solar Plexus	Heart	Throat	Third Eye	Crown
Magnetite	Aventurine Yellow Feldspar	Blue Tourmaline Green Tourmaline	Ruby Peridot	Aqua-marine	Sugilite Opal Clear Kunzite	Clear Quartz

FIGURE 9–11c. Taking Action for Change—Manifesting Your Goals.

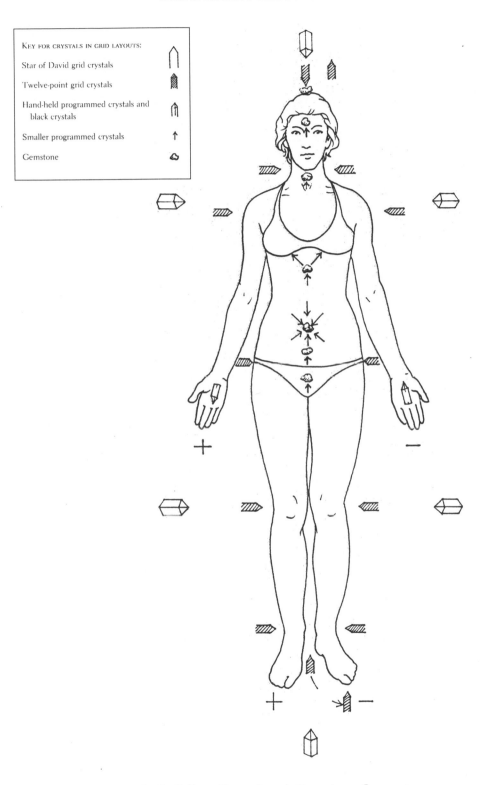

Key for crystals in grid layouts:

Star of David grid crystals

Twelve-point grid crystals

Hand-held programmed crystals and
    black crystals

Smaller programmed crystals

Gemstone

FIGURE 9–12. Building Crystal and Gemstone Layout.

FIGURE 9–13. Chakra Affinities for Building and Spiritual Expansion

ROOT	LOWER ABDOMEN	SOLAR PLEXUS	HEART	THROAT	THIRD EYE	CROWN
Amber, 1 Garnet, 1	Amber, 1 Aventurine, 1	Amber, 1 Aventurine, 1	Aquamarine, 2 Aventurine, 2	Aquamarine, 1 Blue Lace Agate, 1	Amazonite, 1 Citrine, 1	Amazonite, 2 Diamond, 1
Gold, 1	Orange Carnelian, 1	Honey Calcite, 1	Emerald, 1	Gold, 1	Diamond, 1	Gold, 1
Magnetite, 1	Yellow Carnelian, 2	Orange Carnelian, 1	Jade, 1	Larimar, 1	Emerald, 2	Iolite, 1
Pyrite, 1	Chrysoprase, 1	Yellow Carnelian, 1	Lavender-pink Kunzite, 1	Blue Tourmaline, 2	Purple Fluorite, 1	Kyanite, 1
Smoky Quartz, 1	Smoky Quartz, 2	Citrine, 1	Peridot, 1		Iolite, 1	Labradorite, 1
Ruby, 1	Orange Sunstone, 1	Chrysoprase, 1	Rose Quartz, 1		Jade, 1	Clear Sapphire, 1
Orange Sunstone, 1	Tiger's Eye, 1	Gold, 1	Ruby, 1		Clear Kunzite, 1	Selenite, 1
Tiger's Eye, 1	Green Tourmaline, 1	Jade, 1	Pink Tourmaline, 1		Kyanite, 1	Sugilite, 2
Black Tourmaline, 1	Pink Tourmaline, 1	Moss Agate, 1	Watermelon Tourmaline, 1		Labradorite, 1	Clear Topaz, 2

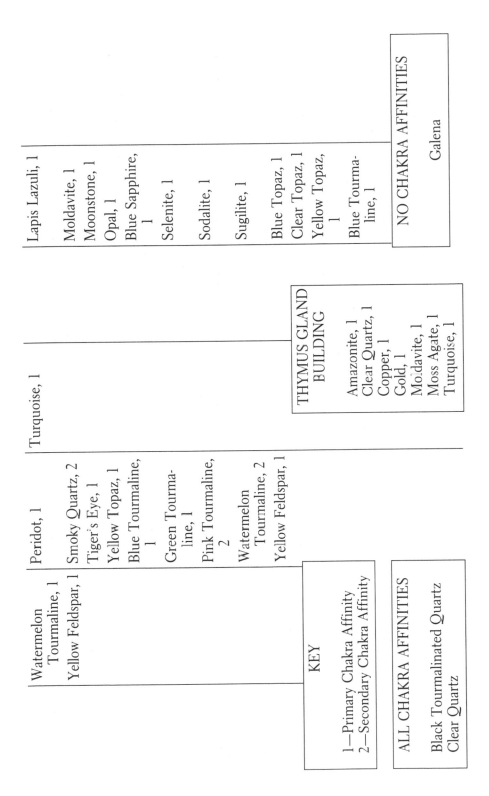

Watermelon Tourmaline, 1
Yellow Feldspar, 1

Peridot, 1
Smoky Quartz, 2
Tiger's Eye, 1
Yellow Topaz, 1
Blue Tourmaline, 1
Green Tourmaline, 1
Pink Tourmaline, 2
Watermelon Tourmaline, 2
Yellow Feldspar, 1

Turquoise, 1

Lapis Lazuli, 1
Moldavite, 1
Moonstone, 1
Opal, 1
Blue Sapphire, 1
Selenite, 1
Sodalite, 1
Sugilite, 1
Blue Topaz, 1
Clear Topaz, 1
Yellow Topaz, 1
Blue Tourmaline, 1

NO CHAKRA AFFINITIES

Galena

THYMUS GLAND BUILDING

Amazonite, 1
Clear Quartz, 1
Copper, 1
Gold, 1
Moldavite, 1
Moss Agate, 1
Turquoise, 1

KEY

1—Primary Chakra Affinity
2—Secondary Chakra Affinity

ALL CHAKRA AFFINITIES

Black Tourmalinated Quartz
Clear Quartz

FIGURE 9–14. Chakra Soul Tones for Building and Spiritual Expansion

ROOT	LOWER ABDOMEN	SOLAR PLEXUS	HEART	THROAT	THIRD EYE	CROWN
Amber, C	Amber, C	Amber, C	Aquamarine, G	Aquamarine, G	Amazonite, A	Amazonite, A
Garnet, C	Aventurine, E	Aventurine, E	Aventurine, E	Blue Lace Agate, G#	Citrine, E	Diamond, B
Gold, E	Orange Carnelian, D	Honey Calcite, D#	Emerald, F	Gold, E	Diamond, B	Gold, E
Magnetite, G#	Yellow Carnelian, D#	Orange Carnelian, D	Jade, E	Larimar, G	Emerald, F	Iolite, B
Pyrite, C	Chrysoprase, D	Yellow Carnelian, D#	Lavender-pink Kunzite, E	Blue Tourmaline, E	Purple Fluorite, A, B	Kyanite, A#
Smoky Quartz, C	Smoky Quartz, C	Citrine, E	Peridot, E		Iolite, B	Labradorite, B
Ruby, F#	Orange Sunstone, D#	Chrysoprase, D	Rose Quartz, F		Jade, E	Clear Sapphire, A#
Orange Sunstone, D#	Tiger's Eye, C#	Gold, E	Ruby, F#		Clear Kunzite, A	Selenite, A#, A
Tiger's Eye, C#	Green Tourmaline, E	Jade, E	Pink Tourmaline, D		Kyanite, A#	Sugilite, A#
	Pink Tourmaline, D	Moss Agate, E	Watermelon Tourmaline, D#, E		Labradorite, B	Clear Topaz, A#

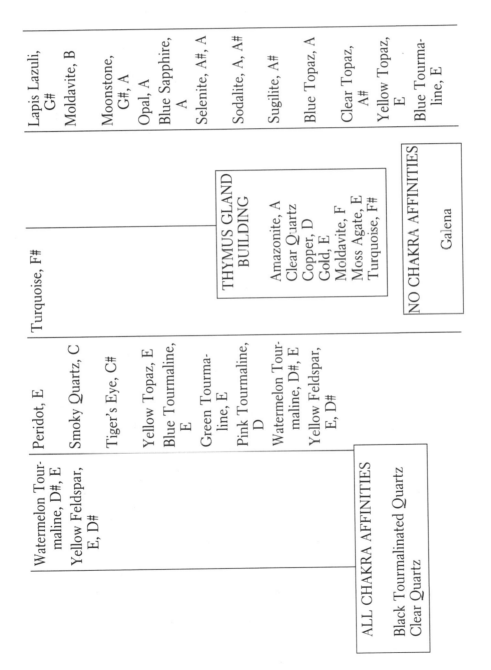

Lapis Lazuli, G#
Moldavite, B
Moonstone, G#, A
Opal, A
Blue Sapphire, A
Selenite, A#, A
Sodalite, A, A#
Sugilite, A#
Blue Topaz, A
Clear Topaz, A#
Yellow Topaz, E
Blue Tourmaline, E

THYMUS GLAND BUILDING

Amazonite, A
Clear Quartz
Copper, D
Gold, E
Moldavite, F
Moss Agate, E
Turquoise, F#

NO CHAKRA AFFINITIES

Galena

Turquoise, F#

Peridot, E
Smoky Quartz, C
Tiger's Eye, C#
Yellow Topaz, E
Blue Tourmaline, E
Green Tourmaline, E
Pink Tourmaline, D
Watermelon Tourmaline, D#, E
Yellow Feldspar, E, D#

Watermelon Tourmaline, D#, E
Yellow Feldspar, E, D#

ALL CHAKRA AFFINITIES

Black Tourmalinated Quartz
Clear Quartz

FIGURE 9–15. Summary of Building Layouts

PURPOSE	ROOT	LOWER ABDOMEN	SOLAR PLEXUS	HEART	THROAT	THIRD EYE	CROWN
Focusing on the Present—Earth	Garnet	Orange→ Carnelian↘ Chrysoprase→	Chrysoprase Yellow Carnelian Aventurine	Jade	Blue Lace Agate	Sodalite Jade	Blue Kyanite
Focusing on the Present—Beginning Again	Black Tourmalinated Quartz Bloodstone	Rhodonite↗ Watermelon Tourmaline→	Chrysoprase Chalcedony Green Tourmaline	Rhodochrosite	Celestite	Blue Sapphire	Clear Quartz
Emotional Balance—Water	Smoky Quartz	Aventurine	Green Tourmaline	Rose Quartz Lavender/ Kunzite→ Emerald→	Aquamarine	Sugilite Blue Sapphire Moonstone	Clear Quartz
Emotional Balance—Accepting Feelings During Change	Magnetite Orange Sunstone Tiger's Eye	Aventurine	Yellow Feldspar Green Tourmaline	Emerald	Blue Lace Agate Aquamarine White Coral	Moonstone	Clear Fluorite
Emotional Balance—Oversensitivity	Smoky Quartz	Green Tourmaline	Moonstone	Jade Watermelon Tourmaline	Blue Lace Agate	Jade	Clear Quartz

	Black Tourmalinated Quartz	Watermelon Tourmaline	Green Tourmaline	Pink Tourmaline	Aquamarine	Moonstone	Clear Quartz
Emotional Balance—Releasing Expectations					Aquamarine	Moonstone	Clear Quartz
Mental Balance—Air	Amber Orange Sunstone	Amber Yellow Feldspar Pink Tourmaline	Peridot Citrine	Emerald Emerald	Larimar (1) Blue Lace Agate (2)	Clear Topaz	Diamond Clear Fluorite
Mental Balance—Manifesting Your Wisdom	Tiger's Eye Orange Sunstone	Orange Carnelian	Blue Tourmaline Jade	Peridot	Aquamarine	Yellow Topaz Citrine	Diamond
Mental Balance—Clarity of Mind	Amber	Yellow Feldspar	Citrine	Jade	Larimar→ Aquamarine / Blue Lace Agate→	Citrine Sodalite	Diamond
Taking Action for Change—Fire	Tiger's Eye	Orange Carnelian Amber	Amber Citrine Peridot	Ruby Peridot	Larimar Aquamarine Blue Lace Agate	Opal→ Blue Sapphire→ Lapis Lazuli→	Clear Sapphire Clear Sapphire Diamond
Taking Action for Change—Manifesting Your Goals, a.	Magnetite Tiger's Eye	Green Tourmaline Green Tourmaline	Jade Citrine	Peridot	Blue Lace Agate Aquamarine	Lapis Diamond	Clear Quartz
Taking Action for Change—Manifesting Your Goals, b.	Magnetite Tiger's Eye	Watermelon Tourmaline	Yellow Feldspar	Ruby Peridot	Blue Lace Agate	Clear Kunzite	Clear Quartz
Taking Action for Change—Manifesting Your Goals, c.	Magnetite	Aventurine Yellow Feldspar	Blue Tourmaline Green Tourmaline	Ruby	Aquamarine	Clear Kunzite Sugilite Opal	Clear Quartz

10 | Meditating with Stones and the Spiritual Expansion Layouts

MEDITATING WITH STONES is a matter of individual inclination. In Chapter 2 we outlined the steps which we follow in becoming familiar with a stone's energies and in contacting the Devas. In this chapter we will give a few more suggestions on this process, as well as on placing stones on the body for meditation.

The use of ritual can become an important part of your spiritual attunement. We have included a description of the Native American Medicine Wheel for those who might like to work with this form. Creating your own ceremonies is a way of creating yourself, and it is not necessary for your rituals to be like those of anyone else. However, it is also true that if you work with a particular form such as the Medicine Wheel, you will tap into the thought-energies of others who have focused on this form. This added spiritual power can be of benefit.

Finally, we have included two layouts for spiritual expansion whenever you wish to involve all the chakras in meditation.

226

PLACING STONES ON THE BODY FOR MEDITATION

Before you begin a meditation it can be helpful to take the essence of the gemstone you plan to work with. Toning its soul tone will amplify the stone's spiritual qualities and prepare your subtle bodies to receive higher frequencies. You can then tone your own soul tone to further attune the stone to your energy system and to balance your energy bodies. You can feel the effects of a stone when you hold it or when you place it on an altar near you.

Here are several more possibilities for the third eye and crown:

1. Place the stone at your third eye. You can amplify it with a single or doubly terminated clear quartz crystal. You can also place a single or doubly terminated clear quartz crystal that has been treated with the essence at the crown.

FIGURE 10–1.
Meditation with Gemstone—
Single Crystal

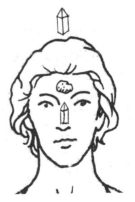

FIGURE 10–2.
Meditation with Gemstone—
2 Crystals

2. A more powerful variation is to utilize two stones at the third eye or crown. Place one at the third eye and one at the crown. Surround the crown stone with a Star of David grid of six single or doubly terminated crystals that have been treated with the gem essence.

FIGURE 10–3. Meditation with (2) Gemstones and (6) Crystals.

After a meditative experience it is important to allow time for a reintegration of your energies. You can hold a grounding stone such as galena to help you focus your energies. It also helps to write about your experiences rather than verbalizing them. In this way you retain more of the quality of the energy. If you also try to express what you have learned in your everyday life, your experience will be enriched.

THE MEDICINE WHEEL

Meditating with the Medicine Wheel is a wonderful way to let the stones speak to you about what the cycles of nature teach us about our own growth. An excellent resource on the medicine wheel is *The Medicine Wheel—Earth Astrology*, by Sun Bear and Wabun.[1] Spring is associated with the East and the Air Element. It is a time of vision, new ideas, and expansion in new directions. Summer belongs to the South and the Fire Element. Action and the expression of will, trust, and growth are the keynotes here. Fall is given to the West and to Water, because it is a time of harvest, assimilation, sensitive understanding, and flowing with change. Like the Water Element, it is a more receptive time. Finally, we come to Winter, which is associated with the North and the Earth Element. Winter is a time of focusing inward and letting go, and of emptiness to make room for new ideas to come. Paradoxically, we are most aware of form at this time (namely our physical bodies), and in order for change to occur we must let go of old forms. The Earth teaches us her stability even in her constant changing.

It is a powerful experience to make your own personal Medicine Wheel of any size. You can use rocks from your backyard, from a special place, or you can work with your gemstones. You will need thirty-one stones in all:

1.   Ask each stone if it would like to be part of a Medicine Wheel and intuitively determine the answer.

2.   Using a compass, place a stone at each of the four directions, to make the cardinal points of the circumference of the circle.

3.   Lay out two stones between each of the four directional stones so that you have a clock face of twelve stones.

4.   Lay out three stones in a line toward the center from each of the four directions (twelve stones).

5.   Lay out seven stones in a small inner circle in the center.

In the Native American tradition each placement is chosen intuitively; you can give your own meanings to each of the placements.

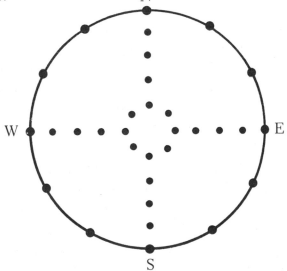

FIGURE 10–4. Medicine Wheel.

When I do a Medicine Wheel meditation I focus on each of the seasons, feeling the movement of the Element. I ask what each season and Element has to share with me now. Then I ask the stone for additional messages. Often I work with imagery to help me connect more deeply. Sometimes I will sense that I am in a particular place in the growth cycle, and sometimes all the places have messages. The rocks will share their wisdom in the context of your practices and beliefs about the Medicine Wheel. The Medicine Wheel is truly an ancient wisdom which attunes you with the connectedness of all life.

INTRODUCTION TO THE SPIRITUAL EXPANSION LAYOUTS

The patterns in this grouping lend themselves to a meditative state in which you activate your spiritual subtle bodies to receive greater spiritual awareness and understanding. As stated earlier, in order to integrate the energy with your mental, emotional, and etheric subtle bodies, it is best to clear and balance your energies in some way before placing these layouts on the body. You can utilize another layout, such as rutilated quartz on the chakras, or any other suitable practice.

It makes sense to choose the third eye stone first, according to the purpose of your meditation. Then you can choose the layout that is most compatible with that stone and your energies. If you have a second stone, you can place it in the center of a Star of David grid of treated clear quartz crystals, as described in the meditation section. Both layouts can bring about an altered state relatively quickly. *Clear quartz crystal* is a good thymus gland stone for all combinations. With the help of these stones you can anticipate an uplifting, far-reaching journey beyond words.

SPIRITUAL EXPANSION—ACTIVE

The energy of the supporting stones in this layout activates the spiritual subtle bodies in a more fast-moving and intense manner. Citrine at the solar plexus can be combined with both emerald and lavender-pink kunzite. Aventurine is compatible only with lavender-pink kunzite in this layout.

Root	Lower Abdomen	Solar Plexus	Heart	Throat	Third Eye	Crown
Ruby	Amber	Citrine ↖ Aventurine →	Emerald Lavender Kunzite	Aquamarine	Amazonite Labradorite Iolite Purple Fluorite Selenite	Clear Quartz Star of David

FIGURE 10–5. Spiritual Expansion—Active.

SPIRITUAL EXPANSION—GENTLE

The energy of this combination is slower moving and more gently activates the spiritual subtle bodies. Citrine on the solar plexus combines with amazonite and labradorite on the third eye, as in the former layout. Moss agate on the solar plexus combines with moldavite and kyanite on the third eye.

Root	Lower Abdomen	Solar Plexus	Heart	Throat	Third Eye	Crown
Amber	Aventurine	Citrine	Jade Turquoise	Aquamarine	Amazonite Labradorite	Clear Quartz Star of David
Amber	Aventurine	Moss Agate	Turquoise Jade	Aquamarine	Moldavite Kyanite	Star of David

FIGURE 10–6. Spiritual Expansion—Gentle.

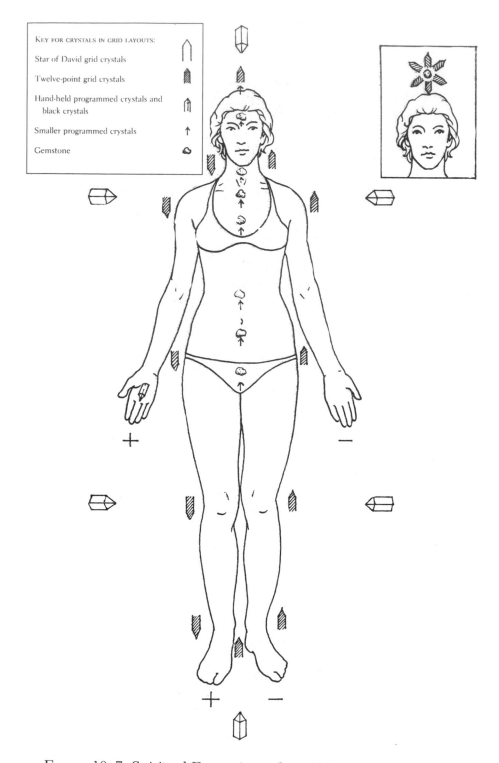

KEY FOR CRYSTALS IN GRID LAYOUTS:

Star of David grid crystals

Twelve-point grid crystals

Hand-held programmed crystals and
    black crystals

Smaller programmed crystals

Gemstone

FIGURE 10–7. Spiritual Expansion—Crystal-Gemstone Layout.

FIGURE 10–8. Summary of Spiritual Expansion Layouts

PURPOSE	ROOT	LOWER ABDOMEN	SOLAR PLEXUS	HEART	THROAT	THIRD EYE	CROWN
Spiritual Expansion —Active	Ruby	Amber	Citrine	Emerald	Aquamarine	Amazonite	Clear Quartz
	Ruby	Amber	Aventurine→	Lavender Kunzite	Aquamarine	Labradorite	Star of David
	Ruby	Amber	Aventurine	Lavender Kunzite	Aquamarine	Iolite	Star of David
	Ruby	Amber	Aventurine	Lavender Kunzite	Aquamarine	Purple Fluorite	Star of David
	Ruby	Amber	Aventurine	Lavender Kunzite	Aquamarine	Selenite	
Spiritual Expansion —Gentle	Amber	Aventurine	Citrine	Jade	Aquamarine	Amazonite	Clear Quartz
	Amber	Aventurine	Citrine	Turquoise		Labradorite	Star of David
	Amber	Aventurine	Moss Agate	Turquoise	Aquamarine	Moldavite	Star of David
				Jade		Kyanite	

11 | Planetary Overview

WE conclude with the messages from the Overlighting Deva of the Mineral Kingdom, and the Overlighting Deva for Planet Earth.

THE OVERLIGHTING DEVA OF THE MINERAL KINGDOM

''The evolutionary cycle of all beings on the Planet is ordered to emphasize the interdependence among all species, both in physical and spiritual development. The spiritual evolutionary cycle can be described as follows: Consciousness manifests in the world of form, in direct connection with the Divine Source. The ability to create with form then evolves, along with the increasing responsibility for the forms created. Finally, Consciousness creates a state of formlessness, totally connected to the Divine Source. A mutually supportive way of being is a necessary condition for all life forms to evolve into their highest level of being. To us, no Kingdom is ever perceived as greater in its inherent capacities than any other.

''The central focus for spiritual evolution in all Kingdoms, including the Human Kingdom, is to serve Planet Earth from a space of Pure Unconditional Love and Light. You of the Human Kingdom have the capacity to create through the use of your mind and will. When these gifts are exercised with due regard for all other life forms, Planet Earth exists in a state of balance and can receive increased spiritual energies. There is abundance present everywhere. When the mind and will of the Human Kingdom are directed toward the satisfying of personal desires rather than consideration of the collective effect on Nature of such actions, this creates imbalanced energies that affect the evolvement of all forms of life.

''The Mineral Kingdom gives service to all of life by providing a stable balance for the planetary structure. The Mineral Kingdom receives its life-force energies from the Sun and from other sources beyond the Planet. All other Kingdoms depend on the form and balance given by the life-force energies of the Mineral Kingdom. You must have a foundation to have life.

''The minerals bring to the Human Kingdom spiritual qualities that can be expressed in human form. Your very physical structure is made up of minerals and therefore can manifest the spiritual qualities of those minerals. Personality and will originate from the minerals and plants that are a part of the physical body. As your awareness changes you can change the vibrational effects which the minerals, as a part of your body, have on your total being. Now you know how deeply you create your reality.

''The Mineral Kingdom evolves through the complexity of form and through the graduating levels of Higher Spiritual Energies. Minerals learn that they can give and receive life-force energies without leaving the space they occupy. This is a lesson of form. There is a transference of energy that takes place as part of the evolutionary process. This may manifest as a new physical structure, or a nonphysical increase in the life-force energy. Just as more human lifestreams are becoming more aware of the time of transition from the present physical reality, so the Spiritual Consciousness of the mineral knows when the time has come to evolve to another level of beingness. It is all a learning process which each life form enacts time and again, toward greater perfection and refinement of the energies of Self.

''Just as the Human Kingdom is capable of receiving from the Mineral Kingdom that which is needed to balance individual energy systems, so too must lifestreams reciprocate in their interrelationship with the other Kingdoms of Nature. Whenever any mineral is displaced from its origin by the Human Kingdom, a void is created that must be filled either by Nature herself or by the Human Kingdom. Balance can be restored, for example, by replacing the minerals taken with new plant life.

''Planet Earth is surrounded by an Energy Light Grid that is the etheric subtle body of the Planet. This Light Grid provides the exterior framework through which Planet Earth's form is maintained. Contained within this outer Grid are Internal Light Grids that are formed through interlocking that takes place among mineral, plant, and animal species at their locations throughout the Planet. The more widely distributed a species is, the greater the Internal Grid pattern it weaves as part of the Planet's structure.

''Fractures or upheavals within the Earth's body, caused by human or natural sources, disconnect the Internal Light Grids. If allowed to continue in this state, imbalance will exist not only in that area, but throughout the Planet, since all energy is One and interconnected. When you hold in your mind the focus of harmony and flow of life-force energies in any imbalanced area, you are helping to bring healing energies and balance the Planet Earth.

''To do this, picture Planet Earth in your third eye with spokes of Pure White Light emanating from her North and South pole areas, and enveloping the Planet in a large ball (see figure 11–1). When you hold this vision in a meditative state with clear quartz crystal, you amplify the external Light Grid that maintains Earth's form. See the energy as a moving rainbow of colors, infusing the earth with the gifts of each ray. The choices that you make in how you give your energy can reflect the same quality of Pure Unconditional Love that is given to you by the Kingdoms of Nature.

FIGURE 11–1. Visualization of Light Grid for Planetary Healing

THE OVERLIGHTING DEVA FOR PLANET EARTH

"Hear my words, beloved lifestreams of my Human Kingdom. I do not condemn or pass any judgment on the actions that you have taken as you continue your stay on my physical body. I am your Mother even as you have mothers in the flesh. My Unconditional Love for each lifestream in the Human Kingdom remains eternally present with you. In times past you were more consciously aware of my needs and therefore took appropriate action to see that they were met. This was possible because you had felt deep inside your being an Unconditional Love for Self that in turn guided you into a right relationship with all life forms, including myself.

"Over a period of time, the overall focus for the Human Kingdom has dramatically changed. You judge yourselves and the world around you. You seek to possess and control things with the goal being to manipulate energy and how and where it is focused. The results of this change in attitude about Self have caused imbalances to manifest in my Plant, Mineral, and Animal Kingdoms. Do you not understand that when you upset the delicate balance in any of Nature's Kingdoms and her Elements that all forms of life, including your own, suffer from your actions?

"Whenever the Human Kingdom chooses not to take responsibility for its effects on other life forms, then Nature and I must step in to re-establish a new balance in the energy fields that operate through my physical body, as well as those that are outside its exterior. No part of me is totally protected when Nature or I initiate changes in the energy. Some areas of my being will experience these changes in a more dramatic way than others. Know, however, that all life forms will experience the effects of our actions.

"Keep in mind that change is inevitable in all things. What I am referring to is the quality and intensity of the actual process of change. Shifts in the land masses are not to be feared. They are a natural process of the perfection and spiritual growth of my being. What you think and feel about changes occurring in any land mass can determine whether you experience this process in some painful manner or whether you go through it with me, feeling and knowing that perfection and healing are taking place within you as well.

''It is true that all imbalances that you experience within the Human Kingdom can be balanced by members of the Mineral, Plant, and Animal Kingdoms.

''You can ensure that my physical body is healthy and supportive of all life forms, including generations of your offspring. There have always been sufficient energy resources available to meet the needs of all forms of life. You are encouraged to be creative in seeking alternative means of satisfying your energy needs. When you give up your self-centeredness towards life itself, then ways of working with energy in a more healthy way will be revealed to you.

''When you speak of Planetary Peace, know, my beloved lifestreams, that this can only be when each of you knows the presence of Unconditional Love within the Heart. All the imbalanced emotional energies, such as hate, anger, jealousy, and greed, can be released so that you experience peace. Love yourself so that your love can then extend to all other forms of life and to me.''

NOTES

1: *Physical Aspects of Gemstones*

1. Wallace G. Richardson and Lenora Huett, *The Spiritual Value of Gemstones* (Marina del Rey, CA: DeVorss & Co., 1980), pp. 16–18.

3: *Learning About Gem Energy: Color, Sound, and Chakra Affinities*

1. Bernard Gunther, *Energy Ecstasy and Your Seven Vital Chakras* (North Hollywood, CA: Newcastle Publishing Co., 1983), p. 78.

2. To obtain a sample pack of color filters (3¼″ × 1½″ × 1″), contact the following:

Rosco   or   Rosco
36 Bush Ave.   135 North Highland Ave.
Port Chester, N.Y. 10573   Hollywood, CA. 90038

3. William David, *The Harmonics of Sound, Color and Vibration* (Marina del Rey, CA: DeVorss & Co., 1980), p. 66.

7: *More Dimensions in Gemstone Healing*

1. John Diamond, M.D., *Life Energy: Unlocking the Hidden Power of Your Emotions to Achieve Total Well-Being.* (New York: Dodd, Mead & Co., 1985), p. 18.

10: *Meditating with Stones and the Spiritual Expansion Layouts*

1. Sun Bear and Wabun, *The Medicine Wheel—Earth Astrology* (Englewood Cliffs, NJ: Prentice-Hall, 1980), pp. 2–3.

BIBLIOGRAPHY

Anderson, B. W. *Gemstones for Everyman.* New York: Van Nostrand Reinhold Co., 1976.

Arem, Joel E. *Color Encyclopedia of Gemstones.* New York: Van Nostrand Reinhold Co., 1987.

The Audubon Society Field Guide to North American Rocks and Minerals. New York: Alfred A. Knopf, Inc., 1978.

David, William. *The Harmonics of Sound, Color and Vibration.* Marina del Rey, CA: DeVorss & Co., 1980.

Desautels, Paul E. *The Gem Collection.* Washington, DC: Smithsonian Institution Press, 1979.

Diamond, John, MD. *Life Energy: Unlocking the Hidden Power of Your Emotions to Achieve Total Well-Being.* New York: Dodd, Mead & Co., 1985.

Gunther, Bernard. *Energy Ecstasy and Your Seven Vital Chakras.* North Hollywood, CA: Newcastle Publishing Co., 1983.

Isaacs, Thelma. *Gemstones, Crystals and Healing.* Black Mountain, NC: Lorien House, 1982.

Keyes, Laurel Elizabeth. *Toning, The Creative Power of the Voice.* Marina del Rey, CA: DeVorss & Co., 1973.

Richardson, Wallace G., and Lenora Huett. *The Spiritual Value of Gemstones.* Marina del Rey, CA: DeVorss & Co., 1980.

Schumann, Walter. *Gemstones of the World.* New York: Sterling Publishing Co., Inc. 1977.

Sun Bear and Wabun. *The Medicine Wheel—Earth Astrology.* New York: Prentice-Hall, 1980.

FOR FURTHER INFORMATION AND TRAINING

Pamela and Jonathan are available for workshops on Crystal and Gemstone Healing. Write:

Pamela Louise Chase and Jonathan Pawlik
2004 Porta Court, N.W.
Olympia, WA 98502

or

Pamela Louise Chase and Jonathan Pawlik
c/o Newcastle Publishing Co.
P.O. Box 7589
Van Nuys, CA 91409